Praise for *The Compassion Revolution*

"Amy reminds us … that we can each embrace the transformative presence of divine love within ourselves."

—Tosha Silver, author of *Outrageous Openness: Letting the Divine Take the Lead*

"Tools and cultivation are all it takes to live the life of your dreams. Amy's book is a literary light that will help illuminate the path to personal greatness."

—Sheila Kelley, actress, TedX Speaker, author, and creator of S Factor

"Amy Leigh Mercree is part cheerleader, part spiritual seer."

—Peggy McColl, *New York Times* bestselling author

"Amy is on a mission to illuminate the path to happiness. She shows us that every small step adds up to big love and joy."

—Linda Joy, bestselling publisher, *Aspire Magazine* and Inspired Living Publishing

"Let Amy be your teacher. She lives and breathes her message of health, happiness, and freedom."

—Shannon Kaiser, joy guru and bestselling author of *Adventures for Your Soul: 21 Ways to Transform Your Habits and Reach Your Full Potential*

"Amy's mission is to help you infuse your life with bliss. We all want more of that! She takes you on a journey to cr⸻ ⸻our terms."

—Chellie C
Daily Af

"Amy Leigh Mercree teaches us all l lives. I love this author."

—Patricia Leavy, PhD, bestselling auth⸻

"Amy is an advocate for self love and self acceptance."

—Molly Ford Beck, founder of smartprettyandawkward.com, co-chair of the organizing committee for the 40 Women to Watch Over 40 awards, writer of the syndicated Recommended Reading print column, which appears in about 70 newspapers across the US, and instructor at General Assembly

"If you are searching for happiness and fulfillment, pick up this book and a jump-start your journey today."

—Dr. Laurie Nadel, bestselling author of *Dr. Laurie Nadel's Sixth Sense: Unlocking You Ultimate Mind Power*

"Amy provides an inspired resource for self-love and happiness."

—Dani DiPirro, author of *The Positively Present Guide to Life: How to Make the Most of Every Moment*

"Amy Leigh Mercree is on a passionate mission to support you in your quest to live life to the fullest! She's your cheerleader plus your guide to access the deepest truths within your soul."

—Kristi Ling, author of *Operation Happiness: The 3-Step Plan to Creating a Life of Lasting Joy, Abundant Energy, and Radical Bliss*

"Filled with suggestions and examples, I believe many people will find exactly what they need to enhance their inner (and outer!) lives through this book."

—Dina Proctor, author of *Madly Chasing Peace: How I Went From Hell to Happy in Nine Minutes a Day*

"*The Compassion Revolution* is a beautiful book that'll inspire profound change in your life, on every level. It'll invite you to speak to yourself and others with more gentleness, relate to yourself and others with more kindness, and show up in the world for yourself and others in a more loving and mindful way. It's time to embrace self-compassion, and this book will help you do just that, and so much more."

—Cassie Mendoza-Jones, author of *You Are Enough*

The
Compassion
REVOLUTION

About the Author

Amy Leigh Mercree's motto is "Live joy. Be kind. Love unconditionally." She counsels women and men in the underrated art of self-love to create happier lives, and she is a bestselling author, media personality, and medical intuitive. Mercree speaks internationally focusing on kindness, joy, and wellness.

Mercree is the bestselling author of *The Spiritual Girl's Guide to Dating, A Little Bit of Chakras* (with Chad Mercree), *Joyful Living, The Chakras and Crystals Cookbook,* and *A Little Bit of Meditation.* She has been featured in *Glamour, Women's Health, Inc., Shape,* and *Soul and Spirit* magazines, *The Huffington Post,* YourTango, MindBodyGreen, and many more.

Check out AmyLeighMercree.com for articles, picture quotes, and quizzes. Mercree is quickly becoming one of the most quoted women on the web. To see what all the buzz is about, follow @AmyLeighMercree on Twitter, Snapchat, and Instagram.

The Compassion REVOLUTION

30 Days *of* Living
from the Heart

Amy Leigh Mercree

Llewellyn Publications
Woodbury, Minnesota

FIRST EDITION
First Printing, 2017

Cover design by Ellen Lawson

Llewellyn Publications is a registered trademark of Llewellyn Worldwide Ltd.

Library of Congress Cataloging-in-Publication Data (Pending)
ISBN: 978-0-7387-5208-2

Llewellyn Worldwide Ltd. does not participate in, endorse, or have any authority or responsibility concerning private business transactions between our authors and the public.

All mail addressed to the author is forwarded but the publisher cannot, unless specifically instructed by the author, give out an address or phone number.

Any Internet references contained in this work are current at publication time, but the publisher cannot guarantee that a specific location will continue to be maintained. Please refer to the publisher's website for links to authors' websites and other sources.

Llewellyn Publications
A Division of Llewellyn Worldwide Ltd.
2143 Wooddale Drive
Woodbury, MN 55125-2989
www.llewellyn.com

Printed in the United States of America

Other Books by Amy Leigh Mercree

A Little Bit of Chakras: An Introduction to Energy Healing
(with Chad Mercree)

A Little Bit of Meditation: An Introduction to Mindfulness

Joyful Living:
101 Ways to Transform Your Spirit and Revitalize Your Life

The Chakras and Crystals Cookbook:
Juices, Sorbets, Smoothies, Salads, and Soups to Empower Your
Energy Centers

The Spiritual Girl's Guide to Dating:
Your Enlightened Path to Love, Sex & Soul Mates

Dedication

This book is dedicated with love and gratitude to the bodhi-sattvas of compassion, both physical and nonphysical.

Acknowledgments

I would like to thank my amazing agent, Lisa Hagan, for all her dedication and hard work and for believing in my mission. A big thanks to editors Angela Wix and Lauryn Heineman for seeing the potential of this project and midwifing it into being. Lots of gratitude to the design team at Llewellyn for their attention to detail and talent. Many thanks to designers Donna Burch-Brown, Ellen Lawson, and other professionals who helped bring this book to life. And lots of gratitude to Vanessa Wright for an amazing publicity and outreach campaign.

It truly takes a village to create a clear, beautiful, concise, and artful book, and the team at Llewellyn is top-notch. I'm grateful for all the blessings that the creation of this book has brought and will bring in the years to come. It was created with love.

Contents

Introduction

Every day we are barraged with slick messaging telling us that we should look a certain way because we aren't attractive enough. That we better get that gym equipment or face cream ASAP. This same messaging tells us, "Quick! Get that new car! Then you'll have more status than your neighbor. Park that glossy new Beemer in your driveway and you'll be worthy."

The thing about consumer culture is that it is all about getting more, as fast as you can, to fill the emptiness and out-compete others. In the rush to be better, we get caught in an endless competition in which we forget that who we are comes from our core, not our outer adornments. There is an abundance of powerful programming out there that tells us to stay in the race to the top. And we all feel it in different ways.

The path to transcending that mentality is being compassionate. We don't necessarily have to reject all that stimulating media. We simply need to bring awareness to the power of being kind! Caring about others is basic, and it's our true nature. Now is the time to return to our innate kind nature. I created *The Compassion Revolution* to make a thirty-day commitment to explore this idea and to share it with you. Together we learn about ourselves, our family and friends, and our world. My hope is that every day you and I make a positive impact on someone's day, including our own. Let the compassion revolution begin!

Choosing Compassion

Being compassionate seems like a pretty simple concept. Just be nice to people and get on with it, right? That's certainly a start. But it's only the beginning of a beautiful, fun, and deeply profound journey. Not everyone will want to take this journey just yet. In time, though, this movement will grow. In fact, it already is growing. Around the world, people are being kind to each other, to the environment, and to themselves every day. Every day billions of people love someone. Out of love, caring is born. And from caring, kindness springs forth.

Cultivating compassion is a path of happiness and self-awareness. It might not seem like the easy path all of the time. It takes effort not to go off on someone who spills coffee on you when you've been having a bad day. Or to bring awareness to what you type in the comments of someone's blog so that you express your opinion kindly and consciously instead of trolling and being anonymously snide.

The thing about choosing compassion is that it creeps up on you. You start thinking more kindly. Negative self-talk begins to lessen. A spirit of goodness comes over you. Humanity doesn't seem as much like a germy mass of self-absorption. You notice the shy smiles directed your way, the doors held, and the helping hands offered, and you start offering the hand up sometimes. Meaning evolves out of awareness and conscious choice of focus.

Choosing compassion directly improves the quality of your energy by raising your vibration. When we talk about energy, we mean the light and energetic particles in and around your body. You hear about when someone says a place has a good vibe or a bad vibe. This is energy. And your vibe attracts your tribe. It shapes your life. A compassionate vibration creates a compassionate life.

My Story

My name is Amy Leigh Mercree, and I want an end to suffering for all sentient beings. No, this is not an AA meeting for Buddhists. This is one woman's wish for a gentler, more compassionate world. And I bet you have the same wish. Do you want a world where your children can grow up loved, happy, safe, and accepted? Do you want to go out for groceries without worrying about locking your car doors? Do you want to smile openly and not feel like you need an emotional wall of protection? Do you want to turn on the news and see that the only thing happening in the world is diplomatic honoring of varied beliefs? Do you want everyone to work together for a better world instead of competing to be the best? Compassion is the solution to all of these concerns.

From a young age I knew I was different, and as a young child, that was okay. I had a gentle, inner exuberance that was simply authentically me. My inner world was gentle, light, and happy. I remember feeling compassion and kindness for the plants in my yard. In grade school everything changed. I saw more clearly that the way I perceived the world was different from most people. My handwriting was completely illegible, and I could not physically help it. My mind was wired a bit differently than some others. Eventually, I was diagnosed with learning disabilities.

I had a rough time in grade school. Over time, I learned to cope. In sixth grade, although the year was tough, I had a teacher who valued differences, and this helped. In high school, I eventually fit in okay, but it took until college to really face my challenges. Freshman year, I flunked out. The same learning disabilities that had won me ridicule in grade school were stopping me from achieving my goals.

I had to make a change. I found two books—*Driven to Distraction* by Edward M. Hallowell and John J. Ratey about ADHD, and *You Mean I'm Not Lazy, Stupid or Crazy?!* by Kate Kelly and Peggy Ramundo—and they changed my life. What I learned was that I had to embrace my gifts and what made me different and harness them to succeed. I educated myself and conquered my challenges. I made high honors in college and had a successful teaching career for years in which I related to kids with love and compassion and healed the wounded parts of me from childhood by being what I needed back then: a force of compassion, acceptance, and caring. I learned to love myself and celebrate my differences. I found my true happiness through self-compassion, self-love, and finding the gifts in my own uniqueness.

Further healing came when I apprenticed with a medicine woman and then went on to work as a medical intuitive. Eventually, I was ready for a new challenge and discovered that all my unique gifts translated into a high aptitude for heart-based entrepreneurship. My differences paved the path for my success today. For me, everything comes from living from the heart, living joy, being kind, and choosing to love unconditionally as much as I am able. I am driven to share these truths with others, and that is why I write books and speak to groups—to share that living from the heart with compassion is a true source of happiness.

I know that life can be challenging, and we all struggle. We experience great highs and major lows. Many of us feel like outsiders or that we aren't good enough, successful enough, attractive enough. Most of us have been through loss, trauma, hurt, rejection, fear. Ultimately, we keep going and striving to be happy and find fulfillment. Those trials can give us the resolve to commit to the compassion revolution. We can make a better world for ourselves and our children together. Does this sound idealistic? Of course! But so what? I want it. You want it. So let's create it together.

Compassion Is Not Codependence

As someone who puts a good amount of focus on the task of spreading positive energy in her life, I often ask myself the question, is trying to care more good for me? Is it safe? Is it healthy? When someone in my circle whom I care about is suffering, most of the time I cannot help wanting to make it better. And I think this is a normal human response. When we care, we empathize and we naturally feel compassionate. Those of us who feel this way naturally attract people who are somewhat like us. But how do we know how much caring is too much?

The definition of the word "codependence" is relying on another person excessively for emotional or psychological support to the detriment of yourself or another. And the saying "It takes two to tango" really applies here. Because in the dance of codependence, somebody has to be the one who is depended upon. Another part of codependence that bears recognition is that the caretaker in the relationship is the one who is in more control. The caretaker needs to be needed. They need to care-take others to feel relevant or safe. Typically someone like that will find somebody to caretake. And this is not a judgment in any way. We all love to feel needed. We all love to feel that we make a difference in the world. But bringing awareness to doing this in excess can help us become more emotionally healthy and happy.

How do we become this way? Look at yourself and the people in your life who are really caring people. Your family is a good place to start. Contemplate the percentage of time where the caring is helpful. Caring in and of itself is an exemplary quality. But overidentifying with another person and their problems can become a little bit less healthy. That's when we start worrying too much. And that's when we start being too affected by another person's life when it shouldn't actually directly affect us or isn't our burden to carry.

Codependence is not compassion. It is seductive to think it is for those of us who are codependent. It's enticing to think that we are necessary to provide help. It feels good to some people to be needed. We erroneously think that if we are needed, our life has purpose, but in actuality that is not our highest purpose.

Our highest purpose is to be a force of goodness. Our highest purpose is to raise the vibration of wherever we are. And compassion definitely falls under that umbrella. Tapping into our highest purpose and being vigilantly self-observant if we tend toward codependence is the way that we can be sure to live a life of compassion and not codependence. One really great way to gauge this is to consider the following: A compassionate act only enhances every aspect of your being. It doesn't drain your energy. It doesn't bum you out. Even if you are doing physical labor as a volunteer, if it is truly compassionate and only enhancing, including to yourself, then you may leave with sore muscles because of all the heavy lifting, but you will still feel enhanced. This is because you will have raised your vibration. And when you raise your vibration, you have more energy. Your mind and heart will feel invigorated and happy. That's how you know it's compassion. With codependence you would feel drained. Every time. Every time you talk to someone, you would then later worry about their welfare or their decisions, how you could help, or what else you could say that might make things better, even though they didn't ask for your help. You end up feeling a little bit depleted. You waste a little bit of your energy on the emotions that are evoked and the mental chatter that you succumb to. That is not enhancing. That is codependent.

That's the difference. When you feel that draining energy, you know it's a codependent situation. When you feel that invigorating energy, you know it's compassion. Be vigilant because if you tend toward codependence, you are probably an empath, which means you easily feel others' emotions. You may be a highly sensitive person. You're certainly a caretaker, and that's okay. The thing about codependence is that instead of helping the other person and helping you, it actually takes away the other person's own responsibility as well as harms you. If you can redirect your caring impulses to the planet, yourself, and the people in your life who are hopefully able to receive it in an equal exchange of positive energy, then you can be a supreme force of good. The caretakers of the world are the ones who care enough to make the effort to make it better. So embrace that side of yourself with awareness so that you can healthily live from your authentic state of compassion.

Mental Health Is Paramount

Your mental health is crucially important. In your quest to be compassionate if you feel off-balance or emotionally confused, please seek the help of a trained professional. This book is not meant to take the place of your medical or psychiatric care. It is simply a booster, a guide, and a support. You matter, and if you are dealing with major challenges like depression or anxiety, please find the help you need so you can feel good again.

Thirty Days for Peace

What we are really talking about in this book is creating a better world step by step and day by day. It is a team effort, but it can start with just one person. So join me in devoting thirty days to peace and compassion on the planet. Each day we will focus on a theme relating to compassion, ending with a practice you can take to heart. For part of the book we will focus on showing ourselves compassion. When we can treat ourselves with kindness and compassion, it's easier to be kind to others. And when others are treated kindly, they're better able to see the good in themselves, and then they start treating themselves and others with kindness. Like ripples in a pond, that kindness and compassion can spread out to entire communities. Eventually, those ripples can spread over the entire world. But we have to start with ourselves. It's that important!

We will also focus on creating a better world through compassion bit by bit. We'll be expanding the messages and activities we learn by being compassionate to ourselves and applying them to our relationships with our loved ones, our acquaintances, and the strangers we meet as we go about our lives. Let's jump into our thirty days for peace right now. It will be fun! It will be transformative. And it will illuminate our lives.

Share the compassion revolution movement with your friends and family and expand the energy of compassion through the world. At the end of each chapter you will find a compassion revolution quote designed to center you in the concept for that day and also to be shared on social media. I recommend keeping a journal as a tool for the journey. You can tweet me at @Amy LeighMercree using #thecompassionrevolution and compare notes. I want to hear about your experiences! Let's spread the love worldwide!

Compassion Affirmations

Before we dive into our thirty-day practice, I want to briefly share a practice that you can easily make use of, no matter what theme or day you find yourself focusing on. Affirmations are wonderful tools. Affirmative statements tell the universe what you want with clarity and purpose. And focusing on the positive is the best way to create the life you desire. I'd like to offer a list of compassion affirmations that you can say whenever the mood strikes you:

- ◆ I choose compassion in each moment.
- ◆ I am conscious and aware.
- ◆ I infuse my compassion practice with pure love.
- ◆ Joy and compassion are my main goals.
- ◆ My sensitivity and empathy serve my highest and best interest.
- ◆ I extend the utmost love and compassion to myself in each moment.
- ◆ I am compassion.
- ◆ My consciousness is woven through with love, joy, and compassion.

It's very powerful to post affirmative statements in your environment. Every time you see print in your environment, you will read it, and so you'll program your mind and cells with the words that you read.

Day 1

Finding Happiness in a Hectic World

Today I feel like life has become a sprint. There is no more jogging. There is no more walking. Now, more than ever in modern history, we are "on" all the time, running as fast as we can to keep up with everyone else. Whether fielding work e-mails during our vacations and evenings or reading breaking news on a smartphone at midnight right before bed and agitating our minds, true rest is less and less prevalent.

More. Faster. Better. These are the new buzzwords. Relaxation is something we have to schedule, and most of us don't get enough of it. The ultimate compassion to ourselves might simply begin with slowing down. Whatever we need to feel whole, to feel good, to feel at peace is the first gift of compassion we must give ourselves, and often the first step is slowing down. We have a hard time receiving self-kindness when we are running through life at breakneck speed.

—— Activity ——
Slow Down to Get More Centered

Here are some suggested ways to slow down:

- Keep smartphones off or on silent after ten at night. Quiet the mind chatter and lessen the screen time for a more relaxed mental space.

- Find your Zen space every day. I like a sunset rollerblading session. Others might like a morning yoga interlude, a quiet walk with a pet, or a mind-clearing spinning class.

- Open your heart to love. Show affection to people in your life and consciously notice when you are being shown affection. Take the time to receive it and savor it. Love is the currency of the divine. Bank it and share it!

- Get your snuggle on! Cuddle up with a pet. Hug a family member or friend. Embrace a significant other. Hug yourself or a pillow. Snuggling is relaxing and releases feel-good chemicals like oxytocin. Studies show it reduces the risk of heart disease and lowers blood pressure. Plus it just feels good!

- Try a weeklong news fast. Do not watch, read, or listen to any news for one week. Experiment and see how you feel. Often this simple step can drastically decrease anxiety. You might notice that a shorter fast is all that is needed to help you de-stress, or you might need a longer break. You might even find that you can vary how much time you take away from the news, depending on how hectic the rest of your life is. Take all the time you need! If it helps you, then you can institute another news fast at times when you feel your anxiety levels rising.

The most important thing to remember is that we have to take time to nurture ourselves. By using any or all of the suggestions for slowing down, we can take a step back and catch our breath, so to speak, mentally and emotionally. And that means that we can remember to take the time to be kind to ourselves.

As an act of self-compassion, tonight I am instituting a ten o'clock technology curfew for myself. I hope it will help me slow down my mind and relax into my heart before bed. Every day I try to open my heart more to love, but sometimes life challenges me or I am too tired or busy. But I realize the easy path is not always the most conscious one. If I take the time to be present and connect when I see my husband for a few minutes at lunch, I may find that a burst of feel-good chemicals are the result. And I hope more relaxed and quality rest will facilitate me taking that extra minute to connect. Do you use your smartphone right up until you fall asleep? How does it affect your ability to give and receive love in real life?

Sometimes the ultimate act of self-compassion
is turning off your phone and looking someone in the eye.
#thecompassionrevolution

Day 2

Releasing the Shackles of Anxiety

Our minds are powerful. They latch on to perceived threats and sometimes focus on them until they deem them neutralized. Unfortunately, in an uncertain world the possible threats are never all gone. Even though we logically know we are safe, our minds can get pretty imaginative and remind us that at any minute a tsunami could cruise into our town and wipe everything out, even if we live in Kansas. We are an amazingly imaginative species. It is one of our unique and valuable qualities, but sometimes it gets out of control.

A twenty-four-hour, in-your-face, global news cycle doesn't help. When our brains first evolved and in the very recent past, we would never hear about the scary events that happened on the other side of the world. We would be concerned with what was happening in our town and in our families. The advances of modern society are fabulous. Almost everything we want is at our fingertips! Life is easier and better than ever before for those of us in the Western world. The downside to that is that we have access to so much more of everything, from new fashions and gadgets to news and gossip. It can be hard to filter out all of the excess. So we need new tools to manage our new and rapidly changing reality and the extra load it places on our nervous system and brain.

Anxiety affects millions of people. In fact, since the 1980s reports of anxiety disorders have increased in the United States by 1,200 percent! In 2011, an estimated 117 million Americans were diagnosed with general anxiety disorder. With a population of 310 million in 2011, roughly 37 percent of America has been dealing with the tension and agitation of anxiety on a regular basis. This is epidemic. And it is time to change it. Self-compassion begins with recognizing this reality, assessing how you are honestly feeling, and then making changes as needed. This may not completely eliminate anxiety and stress, but it can help bring them down to manageable levels, which will give you an increased sense of peace and calm.

Last night, I turned off my phone and computer at ten. I have to admit it was challenging. I like to tweet with people all over the world. I like to see the top trends on Twitter to show me what is happening in the world, and usually right around ten at night I grab my phone and take a peek into the cyber world. My husband was reading the news on his phone, and I couldn't watch a show because that would be technologically stimulating. So, I read a book—it was relaxing and visually stimulating, and it didn't irritate my wrist from holding my phone for too long. It felt like my sleep was more uninterrupted last night, and I definitely fell asleep more easily. What do you like to do

to relax right before bed? Tweet me at @AmyLeighMercree—
just don't be offended if I don't answer after ten!

—— *Activity* ——
Quiet-Time Mantra

Tonight, try to set aside at least thirty minutes before bed for quiet time. That might be reading something happy and relaxing, quietly looking at a magazine, drawing with colored pencils, or meditating. Whatever you choose, make sure that it doesn't involve anything electronic. If you'd like to meditate, you can use a simple mantra to slow down your thoughts for a few minutes before bed.

A mantra is simply a word or series of words repeated over and over with intention as something to focus on besides the chatter of the mind. You can choose anything you like for a mantra. The words "joy" and "peace" are always nice, and the word "love" is a wonderful mantra. Some people who practice yoga like to use Sanskrit words like *om* and *shanti*, which means "peace."

If you choose to meditate, this is a way to slow down your mind before you go to sleep so you can sleep more restfully. Whatever you do before bed, make it restful and relaxing to set the stage for a great night's sleep.

Slowing down your thoughts on a regular basis
is the path to consistent peace of mind.
#thecompassionrevolution

Day 3

Relax Your Heart

Society may not consider it tough or empowering, but we are all sensitive. Every single one of us. We were all sensitive, open children when we were born. Some of us have buried those parts of ourselves, and some of us are still in touch with our sensitivity.

I have been sensitive since I was a kid. My dad often told me to use my "manly powers" to deal with tough stuff. He later shared his concern that I was too sensitive and that I needed to be able to deal with the real world. And his concern was valid. Being an empath and dealing with a loud and brash world still challenges me sometimes. But what I have learned is the more I can embrace my true nature and relax into it, the better I feel. I sometimes have to safeguard my quiet time to process life, but ultimately the more I can open my heart, the more compassion I feel and the more I experience the fulfillment of living.

Relaxing our hearts can soothe the sensitive parts of us. It can soothe the mother who is petrified of her child being hurt and comfort the person pervasively scared of burglars. Relaxing our hearts helps relax our bodies and psyches. It also prepares us to give and receive kindness and compassion. This is an exercise that only takes a few minutes, and it can be done any time you feel stressed or anxious.

—— *Activity* ——
Relaxing Your Heart

Sit or lie down in a quiet spot. Give yourself about ten minutes to do this, including relaxing a bit afterward. Close your eyes and become aware of your breath moving in and out of your mouth. Feel your breath filling your lungs from bottom to top. Inflate your lungs completely and fully. Each time you exhale do it fully and slowly, stretching out the exhalation and completely emptying your lungs. On each inhale refill your lungs even more fully. Let yourself deeply absorb the nourishing oxygen from your breath.

In your mind say "optimum oxygen" three times. This helps your body focus on fully absorbing the oxygen with each deep breath.

Now bring your hands to the center of your chest. Connect to your emotional heart, right in the center of your chest. Feel it pulsing beneath your hands.

Now say aloud to yourself quietly, "I relax my heart." Feel your shoulders let go of your tension and drop gently. Say it again: "I relax my heart." Sense your heart fluttering open a little bit more. Rest in this feeling.

Now one more time say, "I relax my heart." Notice your awareness drop into your heart, like you are present in it. Feel all tension and holding melting down from your heart and out into the floor beneath you. Fill your lungs deeply now and release the air out of your puckered lips. Keep doing this and blow the air out with strength and purpose. Allow the exhalation to come straight from the center of your chest. Keep doing this for a minute or so. When it feels complete, it will subside.

Sense how much lighter your heart feels. Further relax your heart. Let your shoulders relax. Let go into the ocean of love in your heart. Now envision yourself there, floating safely in this ocean. See it stretched before you into infinity. Feel how warm it is, how embracing.

Now, allow yourself to choose kindness in this moment. Relax into kindness. In kindness, there is no judgment, no pressure—just loving acceptance. Feel the infinite love available to you and open your heart to it. It is filled with compassion, and now so are you.

Rest gently for a few minutes until you feel aware of your surroundings again. Rub your hands over your arms, legs, hands, and feet, and really feel yourself present in the room. Then go about your day with the waves of the infinite ocean of love gently lapping inside your heart.

Share your most evocative ocean of love and heart relaxing pictures with us all on Instagram and tag me (@AmyLeigh Mercree), so I can regram them! Do you have a beach picture from a recent seaside adventure that reminds you of the ocean of love? Or a picture of a crystal that gives you a relaxed happy feeling in your heart? Use #thecompassionrevolution and #relaxyourheart in the description so that we can all find each other's pictures.

Relax your heart and let go into
the infinite ocean of love within you.
#thecompassionrevolution

Day 4

A Child's Wisdom

Being compassionate toward myself is a full-time job. If I don't stay conscious of it, I will forget the idea even exists. The life of a writer can be pretty solitary. A good portion of the time it's just me at the laptop typing away, and if I don't make it a point to stay conscious of the time and my comfort, I can tap away the whole day in a state of hyperfocus. I suppose that is one of the gifts of ADHD—hyperfocus. But it also means I will not remember to get up and move around, and I bet you have heard the new phrase being tossed around the Internet, "sitting is the new smoking." A quick act of self-compassion for me is a dance party to a favorite song to get up and moving. I'm going to do that right now!

Whew! Okay, now that I have that out of the way, I'd like to share a friend's experience with you to help you focus deeply on the idea of self-compassion. This example illustrates how listening to your heart and getting clear on what you want are deeply compassionate acts.

Madison's Wisdom

Melanie walked into her apartment weary from a long day at work. She dropped her purse and quietly crept down the hall to find her babies. In their room she found the nanny, Janet, curled up on one of the girls' beds with them, reading a story. Her four- and five-year-old daughters, Mary and Madison, were almost asleep, their chestnut curls framing their delicate faces. She entered and gave each girl a kiss on the forehead and a hug, and they each snuggled into the bed and drifted off.

Janet carefully rose from the bed and Melanie led her quietly out into the living room. She got the rundown of the girls' day and let Janet out the door. She poured herself a glass of wine, threw together a plate of cheese and crackers, and sank into the couch cushions, setting up the Internet TV queue of her favorite shows. She sipped her wine and began to cry quietly. She was gone all day, away from her babies, when all she really wanted was to be with them. But she was alone in this. Only she could provide for them to go to good schools. Only she could curate their lives to be happy. She just wanted to be there to see more of it.

As the tears rolled down her face, she looked up and saw Madison walk into the room with her blankie in tow. Melanie quickly wiped her eyes and tried to hide her tears.

"Mommy, why are you crying?" Madison asked, climbing into Melanie's lap.

Melanie hugged her close. "I just missed you guys today, that's all. I'm okay."

Her blue eyes keenly aware, Madison leaned back and looked at Melanie's face. "No, you're not. You're sad. When I'm sad, I give myself a big hug, just like when you hug me. Then I feel better."

"That's great, sweetheart," Melanie responded, trying to keep a lid on her tears.

"Do it now, Mom," Madison said.

So Melanie did. She hugged herself with her daughter in her lap.

"Now close your eyes and think about something you like. I think of playing tag with Mary in the yard, and then I feel those feelings instead."

Melanie smiled. "Okay."

"What did you pick?" Madison asked.

"I picked when the three of us were picking out pumpkins last month and we jumped in the leaf pile."

"That was fun!" Madison answered. "Do you feel better, Mommy?"

Melanie thought about it and answered honestly, "I do."

Madison threw her arms around Melanie and said, "Good!"

A few days later, Melanie was in her office. It was four o'clock and she knew that the girls were getting home with the nanny about now to play before dinner. The sadness overtook her. She longed to be there with them.

Melanie rose and closed the door to her office. She sat back down in her chair and hugged herself, like Madison had said. Then she thought about running through sprinklers with her friend Nancy and all the kids. She closed her eyes and really put herself there for a couple minutes. The sadness subsided. She realized she was in control of her emotions. And if she could be in control of her emotions, she could be in control of her life.

She composed herself and headed down the hall to her boss's office. Sonia was an imposing woman, all dark hair, dark eyes, and an all-business attitude. Melanie knocked and entered.

"Do you have a couple of minutes?" she asked.

Sonia nodded and gestured to a chair in front of her desk.

Melanie felt clear, hyperaware, and yet almost out of her body. The way she felt when she came up with innovative ideas—in the zone, in the flow. She calmly laid out a plan to leave work in the afternoons and complete her work at home later in the evenings, including all the specific reasons why that would work.

Melanie waited while Sonia sat stone-faced, hopefully considering her proposal. After a minute or so, Sonia said, "I think that could work. Why don't you try it in a trial basis for one month, and as long as everything is getting done with the same efficiency, we can make it permanent."

Melanie thanked her and hurried out before Sonia changed her mind or Melanie started weeping from sheer relief. It had worked! Now, she could see her babies and keep her standing at the job she actually loved. Yes, she would miss a lot of TV, but she had found a way to be kind to herself by taking action to fulfill her needs and wants. She could pick up the kids at school and spend the rest of the day with them. Then after she put them to bed, she could complete her work. It was perfect.

Weeks later, things had been going well and Sonia had signed off on the permanent change. Melanie glanced back at the girls behind her in the car one afternoon. She smiled as they chatted to each other in their special language. Then she heard Madison say, "And Mommy's not sad from missing us now."

A quick heat rushed through Melanie's body, the poignant moment hitting close to her heart. She exhaled and thought about how she was there to hear these conversations now. She wasn't sad—just grateful—and what a perceptive little daughter she had.

"Right, Mommy? You're not sad anymore, are you?" Madison called.

"No, sweetie, I'm not. I'm very happy to spend more time with you girls." And she really, really was.

***

In the story, Melanie had to reach an emotional breaking point to choose to take action and change her life. She was also helped by effective techniques that her five-year-old happened to share with her: hugging yourself to release endorphins and creative visualization. Sometimes these boosts in feel-good chemicals give the needed nudge to take action. It is compassionate to lessen or eliminate your own suffering. It is, in fact, a first step in the compassion revolution. Kindness to yourself translates into kindness for others later in the day or week. Value and respect yourself, and you will be a model of compassion for others. You will be full of life and light so you can share your bounty with others.

Reflecting

Your activity today is just to reflect on the example shared in this chapter. Does it resonate for you? Are there any parts of the story that you can see yourself in? How can you best listen to your heart and have compassion for yourself and others? You can write about this in your journal if you feel so moved.

The love you share with yourself
pays immediate and lifelong dividends of peace.
#thecompassionrevolution

Day 5

Self-Talk Is the Most Important Force in Your Life

What you tell yourself about your life and experiences shapes your world. Telling yourself that something you just experienced was fun, interesting, boring, or annoying will literally change your mood. Let's say you went to a lecture. You could sit there and watch with skeptical eyes, notice all the flaws in the presentation, and get aggravated and agitated, or you could be open to the moment and simply start with kind eyes. You might like it, you might not. From a kind perspective, either is just fine.

When you find yourself noticing the presenter's wrinkly or fur-covered clothes, you have a choice before you within your own psyche: you could judge that they were running late that morning and aren't punctual, and how can they be giving a talk on marketing if they aren't even punctual? Or you could put your psyche in check and instead choose kind thoughts. In that case you might just notice the wrinkles and move on. No drama, no agitation, and, most importantly, no looming fear that someday *you* might be the one with the wrinkled pants being judged as unprofessional. You can short-circuit much of your tension, fear, and anxiety by being kind and choosing to think kind thoughts.

What you tell yourself *about yourself* shapes how you feel about your world. If you constantly tell yourself in your mind how you need to be better—do more at work, be a more involved parent, get in better shape, make more dates with old friends, and an endless list of other things—you will drive yourself toward anxiousness and tension. Yes, it might be good for you to do some of those things. However, if you are equating your self-concept with an endless list of things to make you better you are missing a vital truth. You are perfect just as you are. On the inside.

Inside you are a treasure worthy of kindness and respect. To be happy you are going to have to accept this and commit to remembering it. If not, your happiness is fleeting and based on external situations largely out of your control.

If your happiness comes from within, the outside world is outside of you and you feel that. You can dance in the light. You can weather the inevitable storms. But inside you are okay. Inside you choose to be kind to your true, radiant self, and the relaxation in your heart lessens the anxiety of a hectic world. You can choose kindness and find greater happiness. Try it now.

——— *Activity* ———
Kindness Is Relaxing

Let yourself sail away on an ocean of kindness. Allow the idea of perpetual kindness to take root in your heart and mind. What would that be like? What if you treated yourself with kindness in each moment? How would that feel?

Relaxing. Your struggle would fall away. Your psyche could take a vacation from telling you to suck in your stomach or work longer hours because you are too lazy. What if you only spoke to yourself, in your mind or aloud about yourself, with kindness?

You have heard the saying "If you don't have anything nice to say, then say nothing at all." Could you do that? Specifically, to and about yourself? Not only can you, but you will also find it is not that difficult. It just takes a little self-observation.

Become aware of the "voice in your head," the one who is reading right now. The one who says things in your mind like "Did I remember to lock the car? Better check. I'll check later. What if I didn't lock it? Maybe I should just do it now. After I finish this…" You know, your inner narrator, in there chattering away to you about everything.

Now, make a conscious decision to respectfully demand that your inner narrator only speak to you with kindness. Define what that means to you now. And actually tell your brain, in no uncertain terms, "We are now choosing kindness, all the time." You may make some missteps along the way, that is perfectly natural. Just dust yourself off, get back on the horse of kindness, and keep galloping toward true happiness. You are getting closer every moment, and mental relaxation is courting you now.

It's also important to be in touch with your true emotions. You never want to repress them or stuff them down deeply. And if anything is ever harming you physically, mentally, emotionally, or spiritually, then you must take action on it and pay attention to it. So when emotions come up, once you are sure that they are not harming you, it's useful to simply observe them and see what they are trying to tell you or get you to notice. If needed, respond constructively to the message they are bringing you. When appropriate, bring your focus back to kindness and compassion.

—— *Activity* ——
Kindness Challenge

Think of an irritating or anxiety-provoking situation in your life. It could be a rift with a coworker. It could be your spouse's ex intruding into your relationship. It could be inner conflict you feel about being annoyed with an aging parent's forgetfulness and erratic moods.

Now, list the problem. Give yourself exactly two minutes to run through how you feel about it. Really let your inner voice go nuts and tell you how important this is. Set a timer. When it goes off, you are done.

Next, on a sheet of paper or a new digital file, list everyone involved, and don't forget yourself. Next to each person's name you are going to list one kindness you can share. And you get two! Get started.

Here are some examples:

Rift with a Coworker Scenario

+ Jill (coworker number one): To be kind to Jill ... Well, this is harder because I am mad at her ... but I could get her a vanilla latte when I go to get coffees tomorrow like I used to. I know that always brightened her afternoon.
+ Tish (coworker number two): To be kind to Tish I could offer to proofread her new proposal tomorrow.
+ Madge (my boss): To be kind to Madge I could thank her for her guidance and support in an appreciative e-mail.
+ Me: To be kind to myself I could take a bubble bath at night after a tough day and put some of my favorite flowers on my desk.

Intruding Ex Scenario

+ The ex: To be kind to my spouse's ex ... That is not something that excites me, but I'll try. I could drum up the kindness to greet her with a smile and a courteous greeting when she comes to pick up their child.

- My spouse: To be kind to my spouse I could give him a hot oil massage, which I know he loves.
- Me: To be kind to myself I could go to dance class to release some of this tension, and I could speak to myself only kindly and really commit to it.

Aging Parent Scenario

- My parent: To be kind to my parent I could give her a foot rub, which I know she loves.
- Me: To be kind to myself I could ask my sister to alternate driving our parent to doctor's appointments with me and talk to a psychotherapist about how sad I feel that my parent is losing her mind, little by little. I guess that is why this is so upsetting.

Now that you have made your list, you get to enact it. Within forty-eight hours, do all the things on the list. Notice how you feel as you do them. Happy? Relaxed? Resentful? Neutral? Under your list, write about each act and how you felt during and after performing it. Enacting kindness in your life is powerful. Watch the changes unfold, and if you are courageous, repeat this activity every week.

If you feel resentful as you do the acts of kindness, it's important to observe that and examine why that might be. Are you coming from a sense of lack, like you don't have enough time and energy to share with others? If so, it might be useful to remind yourself that you have an infinite universe of energy available to power your life.

> *Talk to yourself like a cherished friend.*
> *Treat yourself with love and care.*
> *You are perfect, just as you are.*
> *#thecompassionrevolution*

Day 6

Examining
Self-Compassion from
Different Perspectives

In my thirty-day exploration of what compassion truly is, I wanted to talk to different people whom I thought were really skilled at it. First I talked to best-selling author of the books *Find Your Happy* and *Adventures for Your Soul*, Shannon Kaiser. I chose her because I respect her work immensely, know her well, and admire her compassion skills.

I started out by asking Shannon what self-compassion meant to her. She said, "Self-compassion to me means accepting where you are on the way to where you want to go. It is about being kind to yourself and appreciating your efforts despite results or setbacks." That level of self-acceptance is critical to a happy and successful life. I talked with Shannon before she set off on a six-month trip around the world. She had aspired to do that for a long time and had worked hard to make her dreams come true.

In sharing the concrete ways that she practiced self-compassion in her daily life, she explained that "being thankful is a great form of self-compassion. Appreciating what is going well in life is a good first step, and I also practice self-compassion by speaking kindly to myself. Avoiding negative or degrading self-talk by being gentle and positive with ourselves is key. I love affirmations. Writing compassionate positive messages on note cards and posting them in places you go regularly, such as your bathroom mirror, your nightstand, and office desk, can help a lot. Positive messages like 'I am worthy of my desires' or 'I matter, and the world needs what I have' are great ones to use daily."

Sometimes people sabotage their own efforts at self-compassion. I've been exploring why we sometimes make those choices. Shannon had really profound insight into how to overcome self-sabotage, stating, "I think people feel unworthy of their desires and unworthy of being seen or acknowledged. So this manifests in lack of confidence and self-sabotage. To fix it we can start being more kind and loving to ourselves by the way we talk to ourselves."

We need to know we matter and are worth it, but how can we change these behaviors specifically? "Practice kindness with yourself daily," Shannon shared. "Become aware of the inner critic and fear-based voice in your head. I always say, 'See it. Stop it. Shift it.' See the negative voice, stop it by becoming aware, and then shift it to a more positive one. Many people think self-love is selfish, and many women especially feel unworthy of their desires. We say things like 'Who am I to go after my dream and put myself first?' and 'Who am I to care for myself when my family needs me?' So, yes, there is a little stigma attached to it. When it is misunderstood, it can even be considered narcissistic, which kind, empathetic people fear."

In my explorations of self-compassion I decided to also talk to my good friend Stacy Romillah, who is an acclaimed acupuncturist and educator. I asked her what self-compassion means to her specifically. She said, "Self-compassion naturally happens when one dives deep into self-love and adoration. It encompasses all ways of being and doing that honor oneself as divine, a magnificent gift of creation. Self-kindness happens because of these things. Self-kindness can also be something we do to express our intention of self-love, as we move toward self-acceptance. However you look at it, self-kindness emerges from love. It's an expression of love."

I wondered if a daily ritual focusing on self-compassion would be a good idea and asked Stacy about it because I knew that she is an amazing advocate for self-kindness. She shared her daily routine: "My mornings always begin with gratitude and a *big* stretch in bed! Next comes my hot lemon water drink, then a tea. Breakfast is lovingly eaten. So much of my ritual is *how* I do these things, more than what they are! Each day I engage in some form of exercise because it makes me feel so great. I spend time in nature, listening, smelling, feeling, watching, and appreciating. I choose my foods consciously and feel gratitude as I eat. I have different ways of engaging my feelings, beliefs, and consciousness. Sometimes it's meditation or reading poetry, doing yoga, or simple contemplation. Depending on my day, these can happen anytime! When it comes time for bed, I happily slip into my soft bed. One of my acts of self-kindness is to create a lovely atmosphere in which to sleep. My favorite sheets, down comforters, and feather pillows ... Am I happy because of the self-kindness, or do I express self-kindness because I am happy? Self-kindness is an expression of joy! I cannot help but feel happier when I extend loving respect and adoration to myself. It's like being my own best mama. I feel more encouraged, confident, and worthy when I am kind to myself. When I approach my projects and activities with these feelings, I am naturally much more effective and efficient. I am also much more in tune or intuitive with what needs to be done. This saves tons of time because when I listen to my intuition, I know I am working on the things that are right for me at the time. Magically, this allows for much more serendipity in life!" This idea of self-kindness is not a new one. It goes by lots of names, including self-compassion and self-love. And loving and caring for yourself is a choice that resonates through your entire life. When you apply the idea and the principles of kindness and compassion to yourself, you bring those transformative and alchemical benevolent ideas into your own life.

"What I've realized more and more deeply is that the future is not guaranteed. Every moment is an opportunity to love or not. I know that when my time to pass on arrives, I want to be filled with memories of a life and self well-loved. I've also learned that when self-care and kindness are a priority, everything in life flows more smoothly. It is a relationship with oneself. And we all know that when a relationship is filled with kindness, everyone thrives. No one gets hung up on the details or needing to be right … There is less drama and more bliss. I am a health lifestylist, and when I work with clients, I see that when they don't lovingly care for themselves, signs of dis-ease and unhappiness often show up in their lives in ways that feel heavy and difficult. I also have some clients who are beautiful inspirations and examples of self-kindness for me. Their self-love and kindness show. They look and feel younger, they're healthy and positive, and they deal with life's challenges effectively. They are amazing! These windows into people's lives and health inspire me to make the most of every moment. I'm also a mother, and I see how much my expressions of love help my daughter blossom and glow. How could it be any different when we direct that kind of love toward ourselves?"

It seems that self-kindness and self-compassion spring forth for Stacy from the idea and energy of love. For her, it's kind of a poetic and spiritual choice to be conscious enough to treat oneself with compassion and care. Stacy also shared an example of when she recently made a conscious choice to be compassionate toward herself: "This has been a very challenging year for me. There have been so many changes and challenges. Sometimes I felt scared and hopeless. One day I decided that I had enough of feeling this way. I decided that I love, love, loved my life in all its craziness and unsettled ways—I even wrote that on my whiteboard in my office! Then I poured on the self-kindness. I steeped myself in gratitude. I took a luxuriously long shower, dressed up a bit, and made a delicious dinner. I was starting to feel happier! The next day, the magic began. Serendipity walked alongside me and continues to. I'll see someone I need to call at the store, problems work themselves out, I seem to be in the right place at the right time, and my intuition is heightened. It's been an amazing reminder that the love we extend toward ourselves cannot help but overflow into the world and be reflected back to us. Your relationship with yourself is everything. How you are with yourself will be reflected in your reality. If you want the world to be generous with you, be generous with yourself. If you want the world to be kind and engaging, express kindness toward yourself. When we fill ourselves up first, we have *so* much more energy to share with the world. We can give from a place of fullness that doesn't leave us feeling drained. Gandhi said to 'be the change we want to see.' He wasn't kidding! You will have all that you want when you give yourself all that you want. It really is that easy!"

—— *Activity* ——
Your Version of Self-Compassion

After consulting with Shannon and Stacy, I feel more than ever that self-compassion is an essential step in the quest to live a conscious and spiritual life. It breeds our success and our happiness. So now after having read the perspectives shared here from these women, ask yourself which of the strategies they mentioned you are willing to put into action today. Make notes of one or more in your journal and get started.

> *Speak to yourself with compassion on the inside*
> *and you will radiate peace on the outside.*
> *#thecompassionrevolution*

Day 7

Accepting Ourselves in All Ways

As I woke up this morning I thought about an upcoming interview for my YouTube show this week and if I would ask one of my favorite questions: What advice would you give your eighteen-year-old self? I realized that in the many interviews I've done no one had ever asked me that question. The answer that came to mind was that I would instead make a request to her: take a saliva hormone test every five years starting at age eighteen, and keep the results safe for your future self. Because here I am, in my late thirties, supplementing my changing hormones with bioidentical hormone replacement and guessing in the dark about my normal levels from back in my twenties or early thirties.

I'm left wondering if the exchange I just had with my husband would have been so emotional. It was not a fight exactly, because we aren't big fighters, but something that was moderately emotionally disruptive to my gentle constitution. How can I find compassion for myself and my body in this situation instead of thinking things like "I wish that my body was different and that my hormones supported emotional joy that was less likely to waver in the face of triggers"?

I know it's an opportunity for self-compassion. Is it a cop-out or an important perspective to also say it is a first-world problem? To remind myself that there are women all over the world without any access to health care and clean water, let alone delicate soy and yam compounds to balance their hormonal systems? I acknowledge how amazingly fortunate I am to be healthy, happy, well fed, and clothed and to live in a nice home. So maybe my focuses today need to be gratitude and self-acceptance.

In the face of life's challenges, which may seem massive to us at the time, we have the opportunity to interrupt our habitual thinking and even intercept the emotions that are being triggered by our hormonal systems. One of the top ways to do that is to bring conscious attention to our thoughts and to cultivate gratitude. I bring up my hormonal example because a lot of women have been there. Even if it's not because of unusual hormonal changes, it's just because of our normal cycle. And the fact is our hormones govern so much of the way we experience our emotions. Our emotions to a large extent dictate the way we experience our lives. Sometimes I know I feel like a victim of my own hormonal roller coaster. What I'm suggesting instead is to try the activity on the next page and consciously choose to turn down the volume on the part of the mind that gets triggered to be anxious and critical. That part works on the mental side of the hormonal fluctuations. It's clinically proven time and again that low progesterone, which results in estrogen dominance, creates anxiety. It's a chemical trigger for a mental experience.

The same estrogen dominance and low progesterone that happen at the end of every woman's cycle and are commonly known as PMS can sometimes cause emotional fluctuations—bouts of sadness and crying or bursts of anger. Sometimes as women we feel like we're just holding on for the ride with our emotions. And I know the struggle is real. Something that has helped me is the energy and idea of gratitude. It can be a healing balm for the emotional being. So try the exercise below, whether you're feeling hormonal or not, and see how it affects you.

—— *Activity* ——
Rewire–From Inner Critic to Inner Champion

As you open yourself to compassion, you have an amazing opportunity to rewire your brain and your body. You can retrain your thought patterns. You can depart from having an inner critic and create a supportive champion within. Your body is an incredible machine filled with all the information to correct any imbalances. It is an extraordinarily powerful self-regulating mechanism. You can harness that ability today to rewire your thoughts. You can change your brain.

I have used this exercise with my medical intuitive clients for the past ten years, and many people have experienced major results. Take a few minutes of quiet and try the following:

Create a quiet space and center yourself. State aloud, "I ask that all that transpires in this rewire session be for the very highest good of all life and in accordance with universal natural law (helping all and harming none)." Rub your palms together ten times. This electrifies your hands.

Pause with your hands together in front of your chest and allow the energy in the room to shift. Access your body's meridian system (like rivers of energy in your body) by locating a point on your inner calf, several inches down from your knee, closer to the front of your inner calf. Beginning on your left side, using your pointer and middle fingers, tap the point gently five times while thinking of white sparkling lights in nature. I arrived at this number and technique through years of working with clients as a medical intuitive and noticing what works best.

Repeat on your right side.

Now, on the left side, tap the top corner area of the calf more toward the outside of the leg five times while once again thinking of the white sparkling lights in nature. This accesses small, interwoven nerves throughout the body. Repeat on your right side.

Place your hands on the front of your knees and firmly slide your hands down the front of your shins. Sit straight or lie down and now say with feeling, "I release my inner critic into the pure white light of spirit. I call forth my inner champion from the center of my heart. I allow the essence of my inner champion to fill me wholly and completely. I allow my life to change for the better, and I embrace happiness and health."

Bring your hands up and clap them firmly three times. This clap shifts your paradigm to self-kindness. Now say yes aloud three times. Then say, "It is done."

Sit or lie where you are for a while and rest until you feel back and fully present in your body. Be sure to drink plenty of water for the rest of the day.

Do you have ideas for how we can be more compassionate to ourselves in moments of struggle? Tweet me at @Amy LeighMercree using #thecompassionrevolution, and let's compare notes and talk it out.

Your inner critic is simply a part of you that needs more self-love.
#thecompassionrevolution

Day 8

Kindness and Peak Performance

Self-kindness is a key to peak performance. To really put your heart, soul, and full faculties into something you have to believe in it. You have to authentically care about it. Sure, you can go through the motions, and many people do every day. But why do you think so many end up searching for meaning? They are not authentically in tune with their calling.

Maybe your calling won't always be how you earn money, but at least you can feel it. Authentically. You can live for your soul, as best as you can. The only way this is possible is with self-kindness. If you deny yourself or live for others' expectations, it is not kind to you, and you run the risk of missing the experience of true fulfillment.

Sometimes you have to break out of your conventional or habitual molds to step into your capacity for peak performance. Athletes push themselves, for sure. But for you, as an athlete in your life, fulfillment and happiness can be your goal. And being kind to yourself is the fastest route there.

Aligning with your inner truth and choosing to enact it in the most healthful way will lead you to peak performance in your life. All the trappings of negative self-talk and comparing yourself to invisible foes can fall away. Your compassion for yourself can ignite your ability for peak performance.

—— *Activity* ——
Peak-Performance Primer

Here are three peak-performance tips steeped in kindness for you to try today:

+ Right now, define the three top feelings you long to feel in your life. Some examples are joy, love, excitement, passion, peace, calm, relaxation, bliss, ecstasy, relaxation, happiness, pleasure, freedom, and clarity. You get the picture. What are your top three? Write them down.

+ Now define what they mean and give an example. For instance, "Joy means a pervasive sense of well-being mixed with a burst of happy excitement. An example of joy is running through the sprinkler with my brother."

+ Now list the closest experience you could create in your town tomorrow to go with each item on your list. For instance, "Joy: Since my brother lives in a different state, I can set up a sprinkler and invite my neighbors to run through it with me. To amp it up I will put on really joyful music while they are over." I bet you know what

I am going to say next—go do them! Commit to one this week and the next two within the following week.

Why is this a peak-performance activity? Because it is all about you getting what you want. It's so you get what you need and crave. And that is peak performance in action. If you feel how you want to, then you will be more productive at work, at home, at loving yourself.

*Peak performance happens when we feel loved
and supported from within.
#thecompassionrevolution*

Day 9

The Real Reason Why
Compassion Is Relaxing

In moments of challenge or trial I really see why I created *The Compassion Revolution*. This first half at least is for myself as well as all of you. It's been an intense weekend. Many of you may have read my first book, *The Spiritual Girl's Guide to Dating*. It was all about the system that I created for clients to help them prepare to meet their life partners, but the real magic happened for me when I became the guinea pig. I enacted it and as a result met my husband, who is an amazing blessing of a soul mate in my life.

Fast forward five or six years and we are happy and harmonious 98 percent of the time. Friends say they aspire to be blissful with their spouses like us. But what happens when soul mates disagree? Or don't behave as well as they should? Well, for me, it's harder than it was when I was dating dysfunctional men in my younger years because I have an expectation that this partner is evolved, and I'm sure he has the same expectation about me.

The thing I am noticing is that I need to make sure I do not wrap my sense of emotional safety up in anyone but myself, no matter how amazing my spouse is or what expectations I had. So even though I went through my whole process in the book for single people to bolster their self-love and compassion, I find myself here again, in need of a self-love intensive. Have you felt that way in a relationship?

I think we make a lot of strides, but our core issues come up again and again. So, for me, I am back to banishing self-doubt and fortifying myself with self-compassion.

Creating Emotional Safety for Yourself

Self-kindness and self-compassion create inner connection with you and strengthen your internal foundation of emotional safety. If you are consistently kind to yourself, you get the message: "Whew, I can finally relax. I feel safe within myself." Emotional safety begins to set in and grow. Therefore, you foster an internal environment of self-acceptance. No one knows. It is seemingly invisible. But you know inside that things got a whole lot safer in there, and you can start to relax.

Emotional safety lets you connect more deeply to yourself, and this connection to yourself actually decreases any sense of isolation you may experience. You don't feel alone, because you are connected to your own being in a positive, accepting manner.

Feelings of isolation are one of the things that create anxiety. So when you are kind to yourself, sink into your emotional safety, and feel more connected to yourself, you thereby decrease your isolation and anxiety. You can become comfortable in your own company, which means that you aren't worrying about criticism from yourself or others. After you practice self-kindness for a while, you start to get used to it and relax. You can let go of anxiousness by practicing vigilant, radical, pervasive self-kindness. Get started today!

—— *Activity* ——
Embrace Your Sacredness

Bring your focus to the idea that you are sacred. Sacred means precious, special, and a treasure of true beauty. Integrate the truth that you are sacred by saying aloud, "I am sacred." How does that feel in your body? Notice how it uplifts your body's energy. Set an intention to integrate your sacredness by saying the "I am sacred" affirmation aloud daily. This simple act can help you feel more emotionally safe. Just acknowledging that you are sacred and worthy of respect and kindness can help you make an internal shift.

> *Practice self-compassion and experience*
> *the priceless feeling of emotional safety.*
> *#thecompassionrevolution*

Day 10

You Are the Heroine/Hero

As I continued to integrate the feelings that arose after the disagreement with my husband yesterday, I was struck by how each act of love and compassion for myself made things a little bit better. Yesterday, I took myself on a lovely hike and communed with my spirit helpers. I know technically that part is outside of myself, but I needed a touchstone and my guides have been that for most of my life. It is a gift to be able to feel them. I happen to believe it is a gift everyone has. But I kept coming back to giving *myself* what I felt was lacking in those tough moments with my honey. More acceptance. More tenderness. More unconditional love.

The mythological idea of the hero's or heroine's journey really applies to our inner quest for victory and triumph. It is a symbol of defeating our own demons: self-doubt, self-hatred, self-disgust, feeling like we are not enough. If we can apply our heroic love for ourselves to defeating those demons with self-compassion, we are mastering our own personal quest.

Each and every one of us is the star of our own life. As giving as we may be, our experiences of life revolve around our perceptions. Our experiences shape how we see the world. Our thoughts shape how we expect the world to treat us. And our fears influence our behaviors in large or small ways.

We can choose to be the heroine or the hero. We can decide to be a benevolent, daring, kind star who spreads goodness. We can embody the archetype of the hero or heroine who saves the day and defeats evil.

In our own fairy tale, life, we can slay the dragons of our fears and limitations and triumph over obstacles to be victorious. Here's how: be kind to ourselves. So simple. With self-kindness, the evil fears with which our psyches try to torment and sabotage us dissolve. With self-kindness, our limitations lessen, and the endless possibilities of life open up before us. With self-kindness, we can choose to let go of fear and step into love.

In the words of Jamie Eslinger of thepromise365.com, "Lovemore. Fearless." Be fearless today by loving yourself through self-kindness. Be your own heroine. Be your own hero. It all starts inside you. Triumph. Thrive. Start a kindness revolution within.

Am I Being Kind to Myself?

The paramount importance of the question "Am I being kind to myself?" cannot be stressed enough. That one question and the mindset from which it hails will literally change your life.

Each moment offers an opportunity to be kind to yourself. And each moment offers an opportunity to provide emotional safety and health for yourself. That is what the question can bring to your life if you practice asking it many times per day. And then if you make choices that answer the question with a yes, your life will get better. You will feel happier. Things will flow more smoothly overall.

—— *Activity* ——
Self-Kindness Reminders

Here's how to bring kindness to the details and the big picture. When you start your day, make a commitment to bring your attention back to the question "Am I being kind to myself?" often throughout the day. Post a note on your bathroom mirror with this question written there.

Stick a little note with the same question in one or two other spots like your purse or wallet, a frequently opened desk drawer, or your nightstand. As your day goes on, bring your attention to the question and ask it. Make choices accordingly.

As you focus more on self-kindness, you will sometimes notice that you encounter situations in which you have to make a tough decision: be kind to yourself or do the "right" thing, whether at work, with family, or at home. Sometimes you may notice that demands made on your time, money, or energy are potentially too much. You will make the best decision you can, and you will keep noticing. Maybe next time you will make a different decision. There are no right or wrong answers. Only kindness. You deserve it.

Conclude your day at night by saying the following: "I choose to live in kindness and love, give it unconditionally to myself, and share it with others for the highest good of all life." You can post a little note next to the bed with the statement so that you remember to say it.

Try this exercise for three consecutive days. Notice how it feels in your life. You will feel good overall. Yes, sometimes it may make you be more mindful of how you are treating yourself, which can be uncomfortable once in a while. But the sooner you power through that small hurdle, the sooner you can be feeling good and living kindly and authentically. Choose self-kindness today and every day.

Defeat the demons of self-doubt and self-loathing by being your own hero/heroine of self-compassion.
#thecompassionrevolution

Day 11

Cyber
Self-Compassion

According to a 2013 *Washington Post* article, most of us spend anywhere from five to seven hours per day online, whether on phones, computers, tablets, or smart televisions. This varies by age, and the statistics vary too. But what is agreed upon is this: we spend around a third, if not more, of our waking hours online. And since 2010 that percentage has grown overall every single year.

We do a lot online, from registering our cars, to buying our holiday gifts, to socializing with close friends and acquaintances, to exploring our artistic hobbies and interests. How we treat ourselves online has now become a relevant topic because we put a lot out there for the entire World Wide Web to see every single day.

I may be dating myself, but remember when MTV's *The Real World* came out with the tagline "Find out what happens when people stop being polite and start getting real"? Well, we are all living in a giant virtual crucible, and *The Real World* is now online 24/7. The Internet can sometimes be the place where people stop being polite and start getting very real. In some ways, the Internet is one big stream of the collective consciousness. There are fewer secrets than ever before. So in this teeming online mass of humanity, how can we find compassion, kindness, soul, and positivity? I'll give you a hint: it's an inside job.

Love My Selfie, Love Myself

A selfie is a picture taken of oneself using a digital camera of some type then usually posted on social media. According to Merriam-Webster.com, the first reported usage of the word was all the way back in 2002. Now it is a popular part of the cultural vernacular used commonly in conversation.

The process of snapping a picture of oneself and posting it has become normal and on trend. Love them or hate them, selfies are here to stay. And they are extremely common. In fact, "selfie" was named Oxford's 2013 word of the year! And there have been lots of famous selfies, from Hillary Clinton with Meryl Streep, to Barack Obama with Helle Thorning-Schmidt and David Cameron, to Ellen DeGeneres's famous Oscar-night selfie that was retweeted over two million times. Selfies have become cool and have also been widely ridiculed all in a very short time. They evoke many reactions. Some people cry narcissism, while others see an opportunity to foster self-esteem and be unapologetic about who they are.

The Pew Research Center reports 91 percent of teens have taken a selfie. A survey conducted by PicMonkey finds that 47 percent of adults have admitted to taking an occasional selfie. Additionally, 78 percent of millennials (aged 18–34), 24 percent of 55- to 64-year-olds, and 14 percent of adults over 65 have snapped a digital self-portrait too.

Millennials are the most frequent selfie takers; 40 percent take selfies at least once per week and 10 percent take at least one per day. From grandmas to the youngest smartphone users, people are snapping selfies everywhere. Adults document vacations with selfies, teens document their lives and outfits, and some people use the art form as a digital diary.

To illustrate the public's varied opinions on the concept of selfies, consider the brief 2014 scandal of a fake news story stating that the American Psychiatric Association declared taking too many selfies a disorder. The notable thing was how fast the story went viral. People jumped on the notion, which turned out to be a hoax. Why are we so eager to chastise selfies, call them narcissistic, and even suggest they are unhealthy? Sometimes self-recognition makes people uncomfortable. Maybe self-acceptance and self-recognition are actually healthy. Maybe the selfie generations have the right idea. Fly that selfie flag with pride.

I'll tell you what I see: an amazing opportunity for kindness all around. And since in this section we are talking specifically about self-kindness, embrace your previous selfies. Honor your right to express yourself creatively. Acknowledge how beautiful you are because you simply exist. Too often we are influenced to focus on our appearance. But what about what our bodies can do—run, jump, think, smile, climb, dance, talk, share, learn, laugh, create, skate, swim, surf, play, hug? Selfies can celebrate that we exist and are expressing who we are.

Selfies can illustrate how we feel, and sometimes we want to share that. Seeking connection is natural and healthy when in balance. And expressing our healthy regard for ourselves is positive and sets an amazing example for others to do the same. Because the truth is we are all awesome and worthy of self-love and selfie love.

How to Be Kind to Your Self(ie)

First off, if you post a selfie, no negative self-talk. Speak of or write about yourself only positively. Use it as an opportunity to herald what inspires pride in you. Be yourself. You are amazing just as you are. Commemorate something you are happy about or just celebrate being uniquely you. Have fun and be deaf to everything but the love that might come back. Have confidence: fake it till you make it. Be sure and strong in your post. Love yourself and the world will love you back.

———— *Activity* ————
Post a #LoveSelfie

A love selfie isn't a picture or a status update. It's an attitude of embracing, accepting, and valuing yourself exactly as you are in each moment. It's being 100 percent present with yourself. Try it. In fact, try it now!

Think of something wonderful about yourself. Something like "I am so excited to share my paintings and get to creatively express myself" or "I love making people laugh" or "I try my best every day to spread joy" or "I accept myself with caring and love." Whatever is true for you will be perfect.

Now, snap a selfie. You don't need to make duck lips or suck in your cheeks; just be nicely groomed in a way that affirms your love, caring, and regard for yourself.

Post away! Make your selfie a love selfie and a true expression of your self-kindness.

Make every picture a #loveselfie and fill every moment with soul.
#thecompassionrevolution

Day 12

Liking Me, Liking You

Because we spend so much time online as a culture now, I want to take another chapter to get deep into our addiction to, and love of, social media. I think it's really important to keep looking at these platforms because I want you to really ask yourself how much of your time you spend every day looking at your phone or tablet. How often do you check it? Do you check Instagram in the morning when you wake up? Do you look at Facebook while you're making dinner or even eating? Do you use Snapchat during your lunch hour? Really focus in on how much time we spend on our devices.

I want to go through the three main social media avenues that we spend our time on (Facebook, Twitter, and Instagram) and really look deeply at how we can practice compassion on each platform. Some people might think this topic is just a footnote in the book about compassion, but it really isn't. We spend *so* much time online and don't realize how much our self-concept and our life are linked to the Internet.

Like Yourself on Facebook

On Facebook most of us post things, whether pictures or quotes or ideas. We do this to share a little snapshot of our lives, to promote ourselves, to connect, and yes, for validation. If you are working on validating yourself from the inside, then hopefully you will be using social media in a healthy, balanced way. It can be very entertaining and fun and a great way to stay in touch. But *is* it a source of healthy validation?

When you "like" someone's post they will be glad, to some degree. You know, 'cause of the whole validation thing. Share your likes! And what about "liking" your own posts? Does that sound strange to you? If yes, than I ask you, why? Why is it weird to like something you posted? You curated it. You thought it was good enough to post. It is okay, and in fact good, to like yourself. Sometimes we are given the message to not toot our own horns or to minimize a compliment when it is given, but we can bust that system and proclaim that we like ourselves, and that is actually healthy and normal.

I propose you "like" your own posts. You send the message to yourself that you are liked that way. And you are giving yourself a tiny act of cyber kindness and compassion. Maybe it doesn't matter if it is on trend or off trend to do it. Maybe *you* will start a trend. Because wouldn't it be wonderful if being kind to yourself and liking yourself became a trend?

Tweet Your Truth

Twitter lends itself well to the concise. With only 140 characters to express something, you have to be brief and to the point. It is a perfect forum to express your truth quickly and in a real and authentic way. If you tweet or use any other social media profiles, be yourself. Give yourself the message that you are enough, that you are wonderful. You don't need to embellish and enhance. You don't need to put on airs. By doing that, all you do is undermine your own self-esteem, which later you will have to rebuild, or you won't feel as good about yourself, which negatively effects your quality of life.

Instead, be real. Be the real, authentic you. Unapologetically. Unselfconsciously. Be the real you on Twitter and everywhere you go. You are perfect, exactly as you are. Live that truth!

Finding the Soul in Everything

Being kind to yourself online spans multiple platforms. Instagram provides an interesting metaphor for life. You take pictures to share, and then you can choose to put a filter over them to make them more attractive. The symbolic comparison of who you really are and the veneer you use to appear a certain way is obvious. In some ways we are all trying to live up to the new American dream, except now it is a global dream—to all appear rich, hot, young, and popular. The naturally competitive nature of the human being is sometimes revealed online. But all the grandstanding and competition in the world won't end up making you feel good. It is all another hunt for feel-good brain chemicals like dopamine.

Pretending to be something or someone inauthentic to who you really are doesn't feel good. Ultimately, it undermines your self-concept and gives you the message that you aren't good enough. You better slap a filter on the pic and take some really fun-looking pictures to post so you feel good about how you are appearing online. The question is, is it real? Do you really feel the way you try to appear? There's no judgment here. It is just an invitation to explore this in your heart and mind. Even if the result is just you noticing.

Some of us are online for work too. Social media has become an indispensable marketing tool. In fact, if I am doing my job right, you guys are tweeting and posting about *The Compassion Revolution*. And I am thrilled about it. So even as an author I feel I have a challenge to find an authentic voice that is true to my heart and soul.

That is why I propose we all find the soul in everything. A great place to start that process is with a commitment to compassion. Being truly compassionate to yourself means honoring your authentic soul.

── *Activity* ──
Where Is My Soul?

This activity is designed to help you sense where your soul is located. By knowing where it is located, you can acknowledge and honor it, and it can become a focus for meditation. Relax for a few minutes and explore your inner universe. Find a comfortable place to sit or lie down.

Take a few minutes to calm down, relax, and let go. Focus on your breathing. Feel the chair or couch or bed beneath you. Notice how it feels. Accept its neutral support. It doesn't know you, but it is there physically supporting you.

Place your hands over the center of your chest. Become aware of your heart center. Relax into that awareness. Let go even deeper. Feel your heart center pulsing beneath your hands.

Keep your hands there, and now bring your attention to the center of your forehead, between your eyebrows. Focus there. Relax into that. Feel it pulse.

Now simply allow your heart center and your forehead center to synchronize and entrain. You can say, "Synchronize. Entrain." Allow it to happen and breathe deeply to encourage it.

You may begin to feel pulsing or energy going back and forth between the two areas. That is fine. Just notice it.

Now, ask quietly and gently, "Where is my soul in my body?" You will feel your attention go to the place where your soul is centered in your body.

Bring your hands to rest over that area. Feel a sense of honoring as you acknowledge your soul.

Tell your soul center that you want to make a commitment to kindness and that you want it to help. It will pulse back that it will.

Sit that way for as long as you want. When you are finished, bring your attention to the bottoms of your feet. Rub them.

Feel your attention fully present in your feet. Keep that awareness and move up your body, feeling present in every nook and cranny. Be fully present in your whole body. Say, "I am here now."

Rub your arms, lower legs, hands, and feet. Be present in your body. Notice the room around you. Let the outside world back into your awareness and go on with your day.

As you go forward from this exercise, try to make a point of being authentic in every interaction, whether it's something you post or a comment you make on someone else's post. Go ahead and like your own posts, and don't be afraid to be yourself. Remember that you are not in competition with everyone else on social media or even with yourself. The real you is good enough for everyone.

Find the soul and love in every situation you encounter
and find true happiness.
#thecompassionrevolution

Day 13

Living Kindness

Deciding that you are worthy of respect and compassion is the best thing that will ever happen to you. It's really a form of coming home to yourself. It is a liberation and brings a freedom in the fact that you can trust yourself.

In this chapter, we will focus on your thoughts, your words, and your actions. Everything in your life begins with your thoughts; they shape what you say and what you do. So we will look at these three key areas and how you can bring consciousness and compassion to them by focusing on kindness on a regular basis.

Your Thoughts

Treating yourself with kindness begins in your mind. The more often you think positively about yourself, the easier it gets. And as you get in the habit of positive self-talk, you will start to think positively about others and treat them with kindness as well. Here are some tips to help you on your way: Think compassionately and be vigilant. Really be conscious of watching your thoughts—only think kindly about yourself. When you diverge from compassion, correct your course.

Mistakes are natural. Stay committed to only kind self-talk, and reward yourself for your vigilance. Pat yourself on the back and treat yourself. Keep at it, change your thought patterns, and notice the changes. Keep reminders around to encourage your compassionate thoughts long term and make them a habit.

Your Words

As you get into the habit of thinking compassionately, you also need to vocalize those thoughts. It will help you to hear kindness spoken aloud, no matter the source. It seems to become more real if you can hear the words with your ears, instead of just in your head. It will also change the way others speak about you and about themselves. You can become a role model of self-kindness and compassion for those around you!

Only speak positively about yourself, and stay committed to that intention. Tell your close friends or spouse what you are doing so they can help you remember to speak of yourself with care. This will also remind them that they should be kind in their speech as well.

If you make a mistake, notice it. Try to do better next time. Say something kind and wonderful about yourself to balance out the mistaken comment and reaffirm your self-compassion commitment.

Practice. It might seem strange at first, but keep at it. Soon it will seem strange not to! Notice your old habits. When you are complimented, is your first impulse to deflect it or put yourself down? Instead, just say thank you. Not only is it kind to yourself to acknowledge a compliment, it's kind to the other person also, because you are acknowledging and validating their opinion.

Use positive, affirmative statements regularly to speak of yourself. Say things like "I am so proud of my accomplishments" or "I believe in my creative ideas." Notice how being positive makes your life lighter. Notice if you want more of that, and let it spur you on.

Be a model of kind self-talk for others. They will notice you speaking positively about yourself and see that you are becoming happier, and they will want that feeling for themselves. They may start to follow your example, and the more people are kind to themselves, the kinder they will be to others also.

—— *Activity* ——
Your Actions Matter

Positive thoughts and speech are all good things, but you have to put them into action for them to truly make a change. You need to actively treat yourself with kindness in order to be able to share that kindness with others. Here's how you can get started:

- Start each action with this question: Is this compassionate and caring to me? Only do things that are aligned with your self-respect and kindness.

- Change things that deter you from respecting yourself and from being loving to yourself. For example, ask yourself, "Is it caring to my body for me to eat that ice cream if I am lactose intolerant? Might it be more considerate for me to choose a nondairy dessert option?"

- Only associate with people who are kind to you. If you notice someone is not, either find a way to remedy that (maybe talking to them about it) or do not spend time with them. It's really simple. And you are worth it.

You have the power to choose compassion in each moment. #thecompassionrevolution

Day 14

Believe in Yourself

Consider the compassionate act of caring for yourself. By showing yourself care and consideration, you are being compassionate toward yourself. But what if you feel you can't trust yourself to always make the best choices for your well-being? Then what can you do?

An opportunity arises to examine what might be keeping you from trusting yourself. Is it self-destructive behavior? Is it fear of making poor choices like you did in the past? Is it a lack of empowerment around being able to keep yourself safe and happy?

You need to find ways to answer these questions and remove any thinking errors that keep you from believing that you have the ultimate power in your life. Your choices directly shape your life. And building self-trust is a marathon, not a sprint. It takes years of making good choices to begin to feel confident in your ability to do so on a regular basis, but the effort is worth it! The feeling of being able to trust yourself to make positive choices and care for your health and well-being is an essential piece of self-actualization. You can work on trusting yourself a little bit every day.

—— *Activity* ——
Trust Yourself

Trust is bred from feeling emotionally safe on the inside. It is an important feeling for self-actualization. And yet it is not an absolute either. Trust and emotional safety may take time to grow and root in your being. Take the time to sow those seeds and tend them. Your life will be sweeter and feel better.

Self-care and compassion breed feelings of emotional safety, which leads to self-trust. Try this activity today to build your trust muscle.

Trust in your heart and all will be understood. So close your eyes and take a few moments to relax and feel centered. Bring your awareness to how you are feeling emotionally. Simply notice it. You don't necessarily need to change it. Just be with yourself.

Sense into your feeling nature. Are you generally emotional? Are you more mentally focused? Do situations affect you more than people do or vice versa or both? Get to know your feelings with some introspection by pondering the above questions and observing your behavior and thoughts.

Make a choice to work with your feeling nature. For example, if you know that watching dramatic movies is too intense for you, then let your being trust that you will not subject yourself to that turmoil. What is an emotionally disruptive situation for you?

On a piece of paper write a letter to yourself stating that you are now going to pledge to behave in a way that inspires internal self-trust, and that also includes self-kindness and compassion. Your letter can be any length, but the more loving it is the more your inner being can relax into trust.

Set a reminder in your calendar for one week from today to go back and read your letter and assess if you have held up your trust pledge. Follow through and do it in one week. Correct your course as needed, and revise your letter as needed. Set a reminder for two weeks after that and check again.

Be consistent with your trust-inspiring actions.

Being compassionate can be an exciting exercise
of embracing life if you let it be.
#thecompassionrevolution

Day 15

Self-Compassion
Inspirational Stories

Today, relax and enjoy these two examples of people experiencing self-compassion in action, and let your mind absorb the messages of love and positive action. Notice how the people recognize that they need to make changes in their lives and create a plan to treat themselves with kindness. Recognize that these are ideas I've been sharing with you and that you've been putting into action in your own life. And that's it! No other exercises or activities. Use today's reading as a gentle rest for your brain. Examples and stories of people putting into practice what you're learning can help weave these ideas into the way you think in new and previously uncharted ways.

Gil's Gift for Loafing

Gil rushed from brunch with his friends to the party for his nieces Madison and Mary. His sister, Melanie, was throwing a play-zone pizza party for her kids. He got in there, played with the girls, and had a blast. Next, it was off to racquetball with his buddy John. Then, drinks with Bill who was going through a breakup and begged Gil to come be his wingman. When Gil got home late Sunday night, his phone rang and Jen needed to talk about her life and chat for over an hour. When Gil finally hung up with her, he was exhausted. It was Sunday night and he had to get up for work in six hours.

Loafy, his cat, jumped up on his lap for a minute to say hi. Loafy had always been independent, and he sidled away and curled up next to the radiator, finding a warm and comfy spot. Gil turned out the light and went to bed feeling unsatisfied and unrefreshed. He lay awake, overstimulated, till two in the morning. Having too much to do is a total FWP (first-world problem), he thought. "Get a grip," he told himself.

Gil's week was jam-packed with friends, family, and lots of work, plus his sports leagues and city council meetings. Each night he fell into bed tired and harried. Wednesday, he woke up feeling horrible—stuffed up and sick to his stomach. He had a fever and the flu.

Mandatory downtime ensued. Gil watched TV in semidelirium. He knew he had done this to himself by burning the candle at every possible end. As he lay on the couch he observed Loafy when he couldn't stand any more TV. Loafy always found a pool of sunlight or a puffy nest of pillows to curl up in. He was a comfort-seeking cat through and through.

Loafy also found something to play with whenever he was in the mood. Anything would do. The edge of a pillow, a string hanging off the drapery. Loafy was totally self-centered, Gil realized. It looked pretty good to Gil, who knew he needed to make a change. He'd been feeling unhappy and anxious. Life had become too fast paced.

He made a plan to be a bit more like Loafy and institute some planned downtime. Gil decided that on Sundays and on Tuesday and Thursday nights he would do things for himself. Sleep, he thought wryly, flashing to the late-night phone calls he always answered. Those nights his phone was going on silent.

By the weekend his flu was gone. He had the usual busy Saturday, had a blast with his nieces at the pool, and did a bunch of other things with friends. Sunday he made no plans. That hadn't happened in years. He lazed out and tried to emulate Loafy, making a nest of pillows on the bed and reading the paper with a cup of hazelnut coffee he actually had the time to brew.

Then he thought about comfort and play à la Loafy. Gil had never tried going to the spa. It always sounded a little too girly. But last week John told him how he got a massage and then soaked in the hydrotherapy mineral bath, and it was divine. Gil was intrigued and called to make an appointment. And so the man who never stopped had a Sunday spa day and emerged refreshed, relaxed, and happy. Who knew a day to oneself was such a caring gift? he wondered. Gil pictured his sister's face after telling her he went to the spa and he laughed. That was going to be good.

He arrived home to prepare a recipe he had been wanting to try, and Loafy came to greet him. Gil stooped down to pat him and contentedly said, "Loaf, you really know how to live, man."

Jake's Singing Tractor

Janet worked at the local Montessori preschool in her town and nannied part time after school. She spent six hours a day, five days a week, with her class. Now that it was almost summer they were outside for recess every day, and she got to observe the cornucopia of comedy that the playground provided.

Janet sat at the picnic table in the middle of everything, tracking the kids and making sure they were all having a nice time. Jake and Mary were at the sand table, an elevated sandbox at kid level with rakes, hoes, little shovels, and pails. They were making what looked like a sand town. Mary pulled a little figurine out of her pocket. She said to Jake, "This is Albert." She pulled one out of her other pocket. "And this is Matilda."

Jake reached his hand out and Mary handed him Matilda. "Hi Albert," Jake said, wiggling the figurine toward the one in Mary's hand.

"Oh, Matilda! How nice to see you. Let me give you a tour of the city. Follow me." Mary moved her figurine through the sand piles and Jake made his figurine follow hers.

"I like this part." Jake made his figurine talk and gesture to a big sand pile.

"That's the tractor store. I get my tractors there," said Mary, her figurine moving in time to her words and her warm brown curls blowing in the light breeze.

"Cool! I like tractors!" Jake answered with his figurine.

Janet smiled to herself. She loved watching kids' unstructured, imaginative play. Sometimes it was pretty entertaining too. She scanned the play yard. Everyone was having fun and getting along. Nice. Her focus returned to Jake and Mary's interaction.

Jake was wiggling his figurine and saying to Matilda, "I like to be me. When I feel like I need to drive a tractor, I do it. It makes my heart sing and then my mouth sing." He broke into song. "Tractor, tractor, drive a tractor. Get the dirt and push the dirt. Tractor, tractor."

Mary joined in, moving her figurine up in the air in time with Jake's as they wiggled their hands to the tune. "Tractor, tractor, drive a tractor." They erupted into giggles, and Janet laughed to herself.

Mary ran over, trailed by Jake. "Miss Janet! Hear our song!"

"Tractor, tractor, drive a tractor," the two impish kids sang loudly and giggled.

"I love your song, guys!" Janet said when they were done.

"It's about how Matilda likes tractors, and they make her heart and her mouth sing," said Jake.

"That's awesome that Matilda makes sure to do things she enjoys," Janet said off the cuff.

"Yeah!" Mary said. "I like to paint."

"I like to sing," said Jake.

"I've noticed that about both of you," Janet answered. "That's fun stuff."

The kids ran off toward two open swings and Janet pondered a question. What do I like? she wondered.

She liked Zumba. All dancing, really. Did it make her heart sing? Kind of. Actually, as she thought about it, it did. I will go to Zumba tonight, she thought.

That night after Zumba, Janet was energized. She started going almost every night. Now that she was hardly nannying, it was perfect because she had lots of time, even though she was missing her fun money.

She pictured Mary and Jake singing their tractor song and had an aha moment. What if she was good enough to teach Zumba? There was a teacher-training course. She could try it and, if she liked it, apply to teach. Then she'd have her fun money and her Zumba nights. She got home, got online, and signed up before she changed her mind.

It was done. She was training to be a Zumba teacher. She felt a shiver of apprehension and excitement. Could she do it? Those people were athletes!

The weekend of the training arrived. Janet packed up her gallon of water and protein snacks and headed out. The day was grueling, and she loved every minute of it. The end of the eight-hour day arrived and it had seemed like two hours to her.

Maybe this is what they mean by a runner's high, except it's a Zumba high, she thought. She couldn't wait to do it all over again tomorrow.

At the end of the last day of the training, Janet was talking to Cruise, a stylish teacher who'd driven up from a town to the south. Cruise said, "I'm friends with the owner of the gym on Front Street. It's too far for me to drive, but I know she wants to add more classes. Is that near you?"

"It's a five-minute walk from my house," Janet answered.

"Well, I'll give her your number and tell her how good you are. Expect a call."

Cruise walked away as Janet thanked her. Janet shook her head. Look what happened when she followed what made her heart sing. She said a mental thank you to Jake and Mary for seeding the idea in her mind. Her body thrived on all the dancing and high energy. Her emotions fell into balance with all the endorphins, and her mind cleared and relaxed when she exercised. It was the ultimate physical, emotional, and mental kindness to herself, and she was grateful.

You are a dynamo, and every day offers a choice
to create a life you love.
#thecompassionrevolution

Day 16

Compassion and Yogic Thought

Compassion is an understanding of others' distress and a desire to relieve it, a feeling of wanting to help someone in trouble, and a sympathetic caring and concern for those in need. With these concepts in mind, we recognize and express compassion through our heart chakras, which, when balanced, allow us to connect with and feel love for others. Your heart chakra is the energy center in the center of your chest that is thought to be responsible for the feelings and energy of love and compassion.

The concept of compassion is present in each of the major yogic traditions. Whatever type of yoga you practice, your yoga work will necessarily impact your heart chakra and its ability to give and receive compassion and love. Each yogic tradition approaches compassion from a slightly different angle and can teach you to express and learn about love and empathy in a slightly different way. In every type of practice, you will be encouraged to accept and love yourself and your body at whatever stage you meet it.

There are many yogic traditions, each with its own various offshoots, philosophies, and schools of thought. **Hatha yoga** is the most common tradition of yoga and is viewed as the root of most modern yoga practices. In fact, when people use the word "yoga," they are most often referring to the Hatha philosophies and methods. Introduced in India in the fifteenth century, Hatha yoga involves balancing your mental and physical energies by using *asana*, or poses, to help you build both mental and physical strength. It is also known for its ability to assist with relaxation. Hatha yoga incorporates *dharana* (meditation) and *pranayama* (breathing techniques) to help you harmonize your mental and physical energies and find balance within yourself. Practicing Hatha yoga encourages you to focus on the present moment, which helps you access your empathy and encourages a greater understanding of the world around you as it is, as opposed to how you imagine it to be. If you are guiding your own practice, you can choose asanas that specifically encourage compassion. *Virasana*, or hero pose, is a great asana for the beginning or end of your practice, and invites calm thoughts and positive affirmations as you recognize the beauty of your body. *Dandasana* (the staff) and *paschimottanasana* (seated forward bend) are other simple poses that open your heart and direct positive energy toward those you love. *Setu bandhasana* (the half bridge) opens your chest and activates your heart chakra—the bridge of its name can be seen as a bridge between you and other people, and you can direct energy toward others as you settle into the pose.

Because Hatha yoga is more concerned with intention and energy than the precision of the poses, its very nature encourages self-love and compassion. When you roll out your mat, the first things you should do are congratulate yourself on your decision to practice and meet your body at whatever stage of your journey it happens to be at. So often we see images of women in magazines and on film that make us feel bad about our own bodies. We have to remind ourselves that all bodies of all shapes and sizes are beautiful and that yoga practice is not just for supermodels and pop stars and those whose full-time job is maintaining a photo shoot–ready figure. As you grow more comfortable in your own skin, and more appreciative of your own strength and power, you will be able to give and receive compassion and access a larger consciousness outside of yourself. You'll recognize yourself as a part of the larger universe and will feel connected to a spirit outside of your own. You will also be able to encourage others to recognize their own individual value and help them feel more comfortable in their physical bodies, showing compassion to those who might not always show it to themselves.

For those who are more experienced yoga practitioners, **Ashtanga yoga** (sometimes known as Raja yoga) is a more physically challenging tradition that will push your body to its limits. Ashtanga yoga is similar to **Vinyasa yoga**, which you might see listed as a class at your local studio or gym. You may have even signed up for one of these classes expecting a more common Hatha style of yoga and were surprised at the intensity of the experience once it began! The name *Vinyasa* comes from the Hindu word for "flow," which makes sense because in a Vinyasa class your body will continuously flow from one asana to another in a high-energy sequence of poses that are designed to get your heart pumping and challenge your endurance and strength. Because the styles are so physically demanding, practitioners of both Vinyasa and Ashtanga yoga must be very focused on their breath and on the repetition of their pose sequences. This focus helps reinforce appreciation for their bodies and their work. But while Vinyasa has no specific associated poses, Ashtanga yoga is composed of a series of the same traditional sequences, a choreographed set of routines that date back thousands of years, and will carry you from one pose to the next. This means that in every Ashtanga class, all over the world, you will find the exact same sequences of poses. This commonality also speaks to yoga's relationship to compassion: when we recognize that living beings outside of our everyday lives share the same energies and experiences as we do, we are better able to demonstrate compassion.

Ashtanga yoga was created by Patanjali, the author of the famous *Yoga Sutras*, a book of 195 aphorisms written in India in the second or third century CE. The *Yoga Sutras* outlines the eight main limbs, or tenets, of yoga. These are ethical guidelines, instructions for self-discipline, commitment to poses, utilization of breathing techniques, attention to internal focus, concentration, meditation, and, finally, transcendence. To write the *Yoga Sutras*, Patanjali took preexisting materials about earlier yogic traditions and combined them to create the most well-known philosophies of yoga that we have today. Patanjali's emphasis on compassion is apparent throughout the entire text, especially in the early sections about ethics. In yoga sutra 1.33, Patanjali states, "By cultivating attitudes of friendliness toward the happy, compassion for the unhappy, delight in the virtuous, and disregard toward the wicked, the mind-stuff retains its undisturbed calmness." This quote implies that compassion is a necessary component of self-fulfillment. Until you have worked to balance your relationship with others, you will not find enlightenment within yourself.

Indian yoga master B. K. S. Iyengar, the founder of the **Iyengar** tradition of yoga and one of the foremost teachers of yoga in the world during the twentieth century, interprets Patanjali's yoga sutras in his book *Light on the Yoga Sutras of Patanjali*, which is still widely read by yoga instructors and practitioners. Iyengar sees yoga sutra 1.33 to mean that we should "rejoice with the happy, be compassionate to the sorrowful, friendly to the virtuous, and indifferent to those who live in vice despite our attempts to change them." In his view, compassion is tied directly to acceptance and recognition of other energies, spirits, and consciousnesses outside of our own. We must recognize and take part in the emotions of others, practicing not just sympathy toward what they are feeling, but showing empathy and truly feeling with them. Iyengar's interpretation also emphasizes the need to cultivate acceptance, and work with, rather than against, natural energies and emotions.

The tradition of Iyengar yoga focuses mainly on alignment and uses blocks, blankets, and straps to help practitioners understand the subtleties of each pose. If you have ever been at a yoga class and were offered any sort of equipment to enhance your practice, you were likely working with an instructor who was learning from and practicing the Iyengar tradition. At an Iyengar class, you'll be encouraged to focus on the intricacies of each position as you use the equipment to better understand your body's relationship to each pose. This attention to physical detail carries over into attention to metaphysical detail as well. By fully recognizing the uniqueness and subtleties of every asana, a practitioner of Iyengar yoga is training her brain to recognize individuality and uniqueness in her life outside of her yoga practice as well. You may notice that the ache you feel while standing in the kitchen can be relieved by a forward half-bend, and for the first time allow yourself to tend to your body by taking a break from cooking or cleaning. You also might recognize a coworker's subtle wincing every time she has to lift a heavy object, and your own understanding of your body will lead you to help her take care of hers and offer to help. This crosses over into emotional territory as well: if your husband has been getting on your nerves, after a true Iyengar yoga practice, it should be easier for you to look past the minor annoyances and distinguish what is truly bothering him. A key component of compassion is recognizing the unique circumstances of every individual and being able to understand and empathize with their situations. When you can pay attention to the small details that often go unnoticed, in both your physical body and the energies of yourself and those around you, you are one step closer to living out Patanjali's ideals.

Yin yoga is another tradition of yoga that cultivates compassion through attention to detail. Yin yoga primarily focuses on your joints and consists of holding your body in specific asanas for long periods of time. Though it sounds like a long time, five full minutes is actually the shortest amount of time you might expect to hold a pose while practicing Yin yoga! Needless to say, this school of yoga allows practitioners to develop a heightened awareness of the present moment and forces them to pay attention to their physical and emotional states throughout the yoga session. Holding a pose for an extended period of time is as much an exercise in mental strength as it is in physical strength, and once you've settled into the pose, you will have to take control of both your breathing and your thoughts to fully take advantage of your Yin yoga practice. You are only truly engaging in Yin yoga once your muscles relax completely into the poses, hence the extended period of time you are asked to maintain the asana. The Yin school of yoga discourages straining to get your body into a particular position. Unlike in Iyengar yoga, the emphasis is not on the "correctness" of the pose, but rather the acceptance of the current moment and your ability to focus your thoughts and energies.

The Taoist concepts of yin and yang come into play when examining the tradition of Yin yoga. Yang is associated with the masculine and our efforts to be "right" as we interact with others or find various poses with our bodies. Physically, yang relates to our muscular system and can be found when we stretch our muscles or try to "bulk up." Yin is the more feminine side of the duality and deals with grace and self-acceptance. Physically, yin is closely tied to our connective tissues and flexibility. This means that rather than stretching our muscles and pushing ourselves into poses, we can use the concept of yin to meet our bodies where they are, letting them guide us and encourage us to embrace self-acceptance. Reflecting on the differences between the elements of yin and yang, both of which are necessary to live a balanced and fruitful life, we can see that the yin thoroughly encourages compassion. The practice of Yin yoga promotes openness and self-care, teaching practitioners to appreciate and love themselves, regardless of their level of skill. It also encourages us to focus on intention over perfection, a mentality that comes in handy as we try to exercise compassion in our relationships with others.

The popular tradition of **Kundalini yoga** focuses on awakening energy at the base of the spine to draw up through the chakras, releasing negative energies to make room for positive ones. The practice includes mantras, meditation, and repetition, along with the usual asanas of Hatha yoga. Each chakra is a spinning energy center located along the center of your body and can be opened or closed with specific asanas. The heart chakra, located in the center of the chest, is associated with love and compassion. Choosing poses and reciting affirmations and mantras of the heart chakra can guide your practice to emphasize your cultivation of compassion. When your heart chakra is balanced, compassion will flow freely. As you move into different poses, recite the following affirmations to yourself, either out loud or internally:

- I am open to love and kindness.
- I feel united with all other human beings.
- I am connected to nature and all living things.
- I love and accept myself.

You can also incorporate the mantra associated with the heart chakra into your Kundalini yoga practice to fully encourage compassion. As you find each pose, recite the mantra *yam* and feel your heart opening and your regard for others increasing.

The poses suggested earlier in this chapter that fall under the umbrella of Hatha yoga are also excellent for those practicing Kundalini yoga and hoping to build their compassion. Additionally, specific poses known to balance the heart chakra will bring compassion to your practice. *Ustrasana*, or camel pose, in which you raise your chest to the sky, is a great way to open your heart chakra and encourage compassion. Sphinx pose, cat pose, and fish pose will also directly address your heart chakra and ensure that your energies are positive, which will support your ability to practice and recognize compassion. If you combine these poses with incense or crystals known to balance the heart chakra, like rose or jade, you will be one step closer to balancing your heart chakra and accessing your compassion. Using a green or pink yoga mat also will add to your practice of Kundalini yoga when you want to make compassion your goal.

As you realize the impact of your yoga practice on your ability to express and receive compassion, you'll find yourself more comfortable with your body. You will also be able to understand feelings that may have previously been difficult to deal with, and you'll feel more confident in your interactions with others. Marathon runners and dieters sometimes view yoga as just another way to fit in daily exercise or cross training, but its tradition of strengthening mental fortitude cannot be overlooked. In each yogic tradition, no matter how you practice, you will come away from the mat feeling personally fulfilled and able to appreciate and exercise compassion in all aspects of your life.

Consider trying yoga today if you haven't already. You might go to a yoga class or just find a five-minute yoga video on YouTube. Let your yoga experience open your heart to greater compassion for yourself and others.

—— *Activity* ——
Heart Opener Posture

My favorite kind of yoga is **restorative yoga**. It's very similar to Yin yoga, discussed earlier. And my all-time favorite posture in restorative yoga is the heart opener. To do it, you take one long yoga bolster and place it lengthwise behind you as you sit on the floor with your feet stretched out in front of you. Make sure that the bolster is tight against the base of your spine, and then gently lean back over it with your arms stretched out in a T. You should be face up with the long, rectangular bolster underneath most of your back and your arms stretched out to the sides. You should feel a gentle stretch in your chest.

Place a folded up blanket or yoga block under your head and let yourself relax. You can leave your legs stretched out in front of you, or you can bring them up into a butterfly position by placing the soles of your feet together.

If you do not have a yoga bolster in the house, you can use a long, rectangular pillow or fold up a blanket. Even if you roll it and place it under your spine, it will give you the heart-opening and chest-opening stretch you are looking for.

As you relax in this posture you can repeat the word "love" as a mantra or just relax and follow your breath. Notice the sensations of pulsing or tingling that you might experience in your heart chakra and chest as you let yourself open to greater levels of love.

Choosing to unconditionally love others is a path to deep joy.
#thecompassionrevolution

Day 17

Being Truly Kind Means...

One of the most important ideas at the heart of compassion is kindness. The idea of being kind is inherently compassionate. It is an idea that sparks new positive thoughts, and when put into action, kindness can change the world.

Being truly kind means...

+ Caring for yourself like you would a treasured family member.
+ Being conscious of speaking positively about yourself and others.
+ Giving your time to causes you care about.
+ Treating people with respect and care.
+ Complimenting others and noticing their inner beauty.
+ Listing all of your own wonderful qualities and appreciating who you are.
+ Listening to and enjoying a grandparent's story about his life.
+ Making a call to get a cousin her first job.

- Calling on yourself to be aware of your words and their impact on others.
- Writing positive messages in the sand for others to find.
- Making your favorite meal and treating yourself to a beautiful table setting.
- Consciously choosing to be positive in your dealings with the world.
- Sending a card to a friend.
- Caring for the earth.
- Sending treats to your local volunteer firefighters.
- Knitting blankets for your town's women and children's shelter.
- Bringing your excess canned goods to a food pantry for the hungry.
- Treating yourself gently and lovingly.
- Being caring to yourself, others, and the world.
- Trying your best to be conscious and loving throughout the day.
- Supporting and validating your own dreams.
- Encouraging a friend through a challenging time.

True kindness comes in an infinite number of forms. Kindness can be toward yourself. It can be toward a friend, a family member, a spouse, or a stranger. You can be kind to animals, plants, or institutions. Kindness is an attitude toward oneself and others that is considerate, generous of heart, and gently caring. It springs from caring. Bubbling forth from the heart, kindness can change your day, your life, and your world.

Flavors of kindness include:

+ Kindheartedness: a heart-centered nature that is kind
+ Warmheartedness: a gentle warmth that is sympathetic and kind
+ Affection: feelings of fondness and caring
+ Warmth: affection and enthusiasm
+ Gentleness: tender, mild, and kind qualities
+ Concern: interest and caring
+ Care: liking and affection
+ Consideration: sensitivity and thoughtfulness toward others and oneself
+ Helpfulness: friendly caring and sharing
+ Thoughtfulness: care and concern for others
+ Altruism: thoughtfulness toward others
+ Compassion: empathy, care, sensitivity, and tenderness toward others
+ Understanding: sympathetic awareness and compassion
+ Benevolence: being well-meaning and charitable
+ Friendliness: pleasant, open, and favorable

- Generosity: a spirit of sharing and a readiness to give openly to others
- Charitableness: generous in assisting those in need

—— *Activity* ——
Journal Kindness

Take a minute to think about kindness. Think of how it has changed your life in small or huge ways, not only receiving it but giving it. Ponder people you know who embody it. Let the idea of kindness seep into your heart and soul now. Allow it to enliven your spirit with warmth. Let it proliferate through you and change you from the inside out. Take a few minutes and write about this in your journal. Think about the flavors of kindness and compassion that exist. Let yourself relax and write your thoughts down in your journal. Putting our attention on something helps us create more of it in our lives.

Kindness alchemizes the soul, and a sweeter,
richer life is the delicious result.
#thecompassionrevolution

Day 18

The Magic Ingredient to an Amazing Life

When people are on their deathbed, you never hear about them wishing they'd been more of a jerk or been harder on their kids and family. If anything, there are sentiments like "I should have told my family I loved them more" or "I wish I'd been more compassionate to the people in my life."

We all know compassion is a good thing—in theory. In practice, however, sometimes we forget. Life's irritations and frustrations can get in between us and our natural benevolence. Anger and pain can bring us down and make us fearful. From fear stems lack—thinking we don't or won't have enough. Lack makes us contract in our lives instead of expanding and opening our hands and hearts to the world.

When it comes down to it, the real meaning in our lives is born of love and connection to others and how we have shared ourselves and witnessed others sharing themselves with acceptance and understanding. All the achievements and money are nice and pad the journey with pleasantness and validation, but the true meaning comes from how we have cared for others and felt their caring for us.

Of course, that translates to our friends and family. It also translates to how we relate to the world at large—how we have shared and loved and the kindness we have spread.

The magic ingredient to an amazing life filled with connection, caring, sharing, and true abundance is compassion. It gives meaning to the seemingly meaningless. It brings positive feelings to what appears empty. Compassion takes a beautiful life and makes it sparkle and radiate through the universe.

Compassion creates a heart that is full and open, one that is giving and receiving the beauty of positive emotions. These positive emotions inspire our bodies to release feel-good chemicals. Compassion can be addicting in the best way!

Exploring kindness and compassion will increase your quality of life and the sincerity with which you interact with the world. You will feel more and let your heart open through caring. It's very healing to be kind and let down some of our guard. It means we are acknowledging benevolence in a world that is primarily out of our control. It means we are moving closer to trusting life. It means we are moving closer to love— the magic ingredient to everything.

── *Activity* ──
Deep Compassion

In this activity we are going to go deep into your inner well-spring of compassion. You can imagine this as an endless pool of soft, clear energy in the center of your heart. Today you'll tap into that and access it.

Close your eyes for a moment and place your hands on the center of your chest, your spiritual heart. Take a few deep breaths and calm your mind. Now bring your attention to the center of your chest. Feel it pulsing. Feel your hand powering it up and interacting with it. Feel the love contained within you. Notice the energy there. Is it a color? Just one color? Or many colors? Does it feel more like light, fog, sparkles, liquid, or smoke? Or something else?

Now say aloud or in your mind, "I now connect with my deep inner compassion. And I let it bubble forth to the surface." Notice what that feels like. Does it feel warm, tingly? Like a cool breeze? Take a few minutes and just experience that. You can repeat the word "compassion" like a mantra while you do this.

When you're done, grab your notebook or journal and jot down some notes about what it felt like. Now tap back into that same feeling and ask your heart how you can be compassion in action. Do you need to do anything in particular? Think anything in particular? Make any notes about that.

When that feels complete, thank your heart for allowing you to go deep within and experience that inner compassion. And bring that essence with you back into your day.

Compassion is the magic ingredient to an amazing life.
#thecompassionrevolution

Day 19

Care Like You Have One Day Left

No discussion of compassion for your world would be complete without talking about friends and family. Our friends and family are the glue that holds us together in a world where life has become increasingly impersonal. Our friends and close family members are sometimes our sounding boards, our playmates, and our problem solvers, and sometimes they are just there to listen or cheer us on. And like the champions they are, they provide us with varying levels of unconditional love.

Each time we make friends we risk having our heart hurt. Each time we connect with a new lover or significant other we run the risk of getting hurt. Each time we renew our commitment to our marital partner we risk it. Even in small ways, we are taking a risk every day. Risking our hearts is a courageous action. It is the ultimate strength. Vulnerability is an act of courage. In our culture this has been thwarted by the constant quest for power, status, and money. But the real status is the muscle that we build emotionally. It is the fortitude that we acquire through the ups and downs of life, through the trials and tribulations and richness of the human experience. And as life burnishes and polishes us to a sheen that is more caring and more compassionate through experience, we have the opportunity to shine.

Magic happens when we look to our own core and speak its truth. We learn more about ourselves every time we take this emotional risk. Every time we talk to someone new at our exercise class we take a risk. Every time we push ourselves to take the time to ask a stranger if he or she needs help. Even those moments when we're offering our caring we're still risking rejection. We're wired as humans to avoid what is unpleasant, and rejection is certainly an unpleasant experience.

But what if you realized you only had one day left on this earth? What would that mean for you? Would your day be devoted to all the people you love and care about? Would it be focused on spreading love to as many strangers as possible in one day? Would you care if you are vulnerable? Because the imagined consequences would only be one day long and then would be over?

A life lived with an intention of compassion is a life lived as if it might be over at any time. This is not a sad thing. The soul unfolds continually and eternally. And if you realize there's nothing to fear, then it is all just a gorgeous privilege.

With this fear of mortality released we all have the opportunity to live our lives with a deep intention of compassion in each and every moment. When we release the fear of being rejected or hurt, we free ourselves. We give ourselves the gift of true freedom, and the result is we can give unconditionally. We can love infinitely. We can share eternally with no thought of lack. Emotional lack is simply a limited perception of the boundless love in our universe.

So ask yourself, is the love in our universe infinite? Do you feel love is infinite when you connect with people you care about? Do you feel it when you connect with your spiritual source if you have one? Do you feel it when you connect with your spirit guides? Do you feel it out in nature? Do you feel the feeling of interconnection between you and the entire natural world surrounding you? The idea of living a deeply compassionate life is a spiritual one. And it's not religious. But it is altruistic and full of depth and meaning. Perhaps the intention of living compassionately can give your life on earth meaning.

Take a few minutes and think and feel about what living a compassionate life would look like. If you spent tomorrow with your focus for the day being infinitely compassionate in each moment, what would your day be like? What would your heart feel like?

Now there will be a part of you inside that will say, "Wait, wait! I am going to get hurt. I am risking rejection. This is too risky. I don't know if I can bear it. This much vulnerability is going to hurt too much!" But what if you did it anyway? You would discover that you are infinitely strong. And I suspect you would discover that a life lived from a place of compassion is filled with meaning and joy. And the potential hurt of making yourself emotionally available passes. Especially if you let it simply pass through you instead of grasping at it or avoiding it. The only way to do this is to jump in with both feet.

To be infinitely compassionate in each moment takes relentless awareness of your thoughts, words, and actions. And like anything else, just do the best that you can. Work at it. Most people who do anything worth doing have to work at it at some point. When you practice, it will get easier. So make compassion a priority today.

—— *Activity* ——
Meditation on Compassion

Today, let's do a very simple exercise. I'd like to invite you to meditate on the idea of compassion. I will guide you on how to do this. Find a comfortable spot to sit or lie down. Make sure you are relaxed and that you have at least fifteen minutes to do this activity. Keep a journal nearby, so you can record your thoughts when you finish.

Get comfortable and begin to notice the breath moving in and out of your body. As you breathe in through your nose, bring the breath all the way down into the base of your abdomen and keep filling your lungs from bottom to top when inhale as deep as you possibly can. Then slowly purse your lips (imagine that you have a straw in your mouth) and blow the air out as slowly as possible for as long as possible.

Do this pursed-lips breathing two more times. Take a moment and notice how that feels. Feel if your body is getting more relaxed. Notice if you felt like your lung capacity was a lot greater than you realized. In my work as a medical intuitive one of the things I've learned is that we often hold emotion in the lungs. The traditional emotion that is held in the lungs is grief but also some sadness at times. And these are typically the emotions that we feel when we have experienced rejection in the past. So as you get ready to meditate on compassion, I want you to release the past energies that are not for your highest good. It's so simple. It's just going to happen right now. Do one more deep inhalation, and then exhale with pursed lips. As you do that, in your mind repeat the following sentence three times: "I let go of all past grief and sadness that has been in my lungs and the entirety of my body."

Notice how wonderful that feels. You may feel emotion flowing. The trick with any emotion that you feel, whether it's the highest high or the lowest low or somewhere in between, is to simply let it pass through you. If you grasp it or try to prevent it or change it, then you just end up having to deal with it longer.

Now from your lighter state, you are ready to meditate upon compassion. Place your hands in your lap or in any of the many traditional meditation postures that you might like. You can also just lie down with your hands on your heart.

We are now going to focus on a mantra for about ten minutes. Your mantra is simple: it is the word "compassion." So simply relax and allow your mind to be clear of thoughts. When you feel sensations in your body, simply repeat the word "compassion" and bring yourself back to focus. As you repeat the word, you can bring your attention to the center of your chest. You may also feel your attention at your brow center. Both of these energy centers are way stations for your compassion. It's nice to immerse yourself in these and really let yourself experience the feeling that compassion brings. You may notice colors or textures associated with this feeling. You may notice images or sounds associated with this feeling. Simply notice and keep repeating the mantra. When it's time to stop, simply stop repeating the mantra. If you'd like, you can set a timer for five to ten minutes and then stop when the timer tells you it's time.

After such a meditative experience, I feel like I should tell you namaste!

If you knew today was your last day here,
how would you share your love with the world?
#thecompassionrevolution

Day 20

Compassion for Nurturing and Validation

We are all conditioned to crave validation. Since infancy we have been taught what we can do to get affection, attention, and love. It's human to want all of those things. As much as we think we don't need people to like us and that we are confident how we are, the truth is we are made to seek out validation. Being aware of that is important because then we are less likely to behave unconsciously, and instead we will choose aware and conscious action more often.

Our hearts crave love. We can deny it or suppress it, but deep down we all want to be loved. And being liked is good too, because it is a precursor to love and a nice, mild form of it. We seek connection.

Now that we have stepped online, there are infinite chances for connection twenty-four hours a day, seven days a week. And the human part that wants to connect and be validated has become a kid in a candy store. At times the kid is having fun, getting to try different types of candy, and at times the kid has been eating candy corn for three hours straight and is overstimulated, running around in circles. That's all of us on the Internet at various times.

Being online is a major part of our lives now. We use it for work, entertainment, connection, shopping, finding information—basically everything. And social interaction and connection happen there for us all at varying degrees.

Connecting and being entertained online can be a little bit addicting. In fact, recent studies have shown how dopamine, the neurotransmitter, not only rewards us with a chemical hit when we act but also encourages us to act beforehand, inspiring the thrill of the hunt. Because the Internet is radically quick, we run through this cycle at breakneck speed hundreds of times per day. Seek info. Get info. Seek again. Find again. Each of those gives us a shot of dopamine and signals feedback for expected rewards. It rewards and stimulates us, and quickly we are in a dopamine loop. The Internet makes reward seeking so easy. Sometimes we are hunting heavily, like when scouring online for reviews of the new car we might purchase. Each time we find more information we are spurred forward by dopamine to find more, and the loop continues.

Combine the dopamine loop with our natural human need for validation and we can easily fall down the rabbit hole of social media connection and observation for hours at a time. If someone likes our pin or status update or retweets our musing, we feel the hit that chemically tells us, "They like and approve of me, and it feels good. I want more of that." And we keep hunting for validation that way.

The problem is, just like for the kid in the candy store, the validation we get online is mostly empty calories. It doesn't satisfy us in a meaningful way because it is largely impersonal and most importantly because it is external. External validation only leaves us wanting more. There can never be enough of it.

Like candy, external validation is mostly empty and doesn't nourish us in a meaningful way. We need internal validation that comes from our strong inner foundation. That is what can equip us to thrive and be happy in the diverse and fast-paced life we live.

How the heck do we find validation within? It sounds hard and foreign because our culture and media promote the opposite. In fact, advertisers need you to seek that validation outside yourself to motivate you to buy. There is a lot of money riding on you seeking external validation!

For example, take a cleaning product marketed toward the busy mom. In a commercial another woman might come over, see how clean her house it, praise her, and be a little bit envious. The busy mom is depicted getting a hit of chemical validation. "Oh yeah! My floors are blowing away her floors!" is basically what her very human brain is saying. She likely doesn't even know what is happening inside. She just felt good because she bought that stuff, and the viewer got the neural feedback indicating an anticipated reward while watching, so she might pick that up next time she is at the store.

The same thing goes for the manly truck commercials. The truck is hauling stuff, bouncing over big hills, and driving sleekly down a coastal highway. "Wow, the person who drives that truck is really strong, capable, and masculine, but he has style too," says the ad. The commercial-watching brain replies, "Mmmm, I'd like to feel like that." And it starts sending dopamine in anticipation of the reward. The thing is, the viewer is not enhanced for long. Because after the chemical crash, unless he or she goes out to do something that they think will make people see them as strong, capable, and stylish right away, the feel-good chemicals won't continue. Then he or she might feel the urge to still hunt for validation and hop on social media, unconsciously looking for a hit. The "Ooooh, my tweet got favorited" hit gives the chemical hit, but nobody's life was significantly enhanced.

Instead, you can validate yourself and use social media consciously and moderately. Here's how: choose self-love and demonstrate it to yourself with self-kindness online and in real life. Foster self-love today and feel validated from within.

Self-love starts with self-acceptance. You exist. You are perfect, with all your imperfections. You are exactly right, exactly as you are. Accepting yourself is resting in that knowledge. It requires practice. You will need to notice when you are not accepting yourself and redirect your thoughts and actions.

Compassion Guidelines for Self-Acceptance

+ Be kind to yourself. This demonstrates you are accepting and loving yourself.

+ Only positive self-talk. No "I wish my stomach were flatter" stuff. Instead, try "I love the color of this dress. It feels so vibrant on my body."

+ Be vigilant in your mind. Only kind thoughts toward yourself. Only self-acceptance and loving inner talk. Stop yourself if you start to think, "I have to be better, work more, clean more …" Instead, lovingly and honestly assess the situation. As long as you are being respectful to your housemates, and as long as you are trying your best at work and getting good feedback from your boss, then you are meeting the requirements of your life well. And there is no need to bully yourself and undermine your self-esteem. You are enough. You are great. Catch yourself and redirect your thoughts to something like this: "I am really proud of myself for being responsible and living in a conscious and caring manner toward myself and others."

After you start accepting yourself, you will be more able to take it a step further and love yourself. Loving yourself means unconditionally feeling caring and acceptance toward your being. It means seeing your beauty and goodness and honoring who you are. It means accepting your faults and quirks wholeheartedly and working toward only having that increase your self-love. Self-love takes practice. It takes effort, like a marriage. You do it because you care about your health and well-being. You do it because you love yourself. And you can learn how.

—— *Activity* ——
Amping Up Your Self-Love

Cultivate the same, infinite love for yourself that you feel for a wonderful child or a treasured spouse. Treat yourself with caring. Demonstrate your love for yourself in large and small ways to show your inner soul that it is loved and can feel safe, exactly as it is, all of the time. Try these self-love practices:

1. Post a list of three affirmative statements that proclaim your love for yourself. This can go on the bathroom mirror or near your bed.

   Here are some suggestions:

   - I love myself in every moment, exactly as I am.
   - I treasure myself and my precious heart.
   - I am worthy of respect, love, and kindness at all times and behave as such.

2. Say those statements aloud in the morning and evening. After waking and before sleeping are good times. Make a commitment to do this.

3. Commit to taking yourself on one special self-love adventure per week. It might be as simple as getting a fresh juice and going for a walk or as extravagant as tak-

ing a road trip to the beach or the spa. On this adventure, make sure you take a few minutes in your mental space to consciously do some self-love talk. Say things like "I am so glad I get to treat myself. I don't need a reason, and it's not based on anything. I do it simply because I exist and I love myself" and "I really love myself, my quirks, my flaws, my talents, and my opinions. I value who I am and validate myself."

Self-love will validate you and fill that need within. You can fill the emptiness from within with love and kindness and feel better. Self-kindness validates you in a way that your soul and heart can understand and appreciate. Emotional health will result.

Here are some self-love pointers:

- You are worthy of love.
- You are worthy of self-love.
- You are perfect, just as you are, on the inside.
- You deserve kindness.
- You can choose kindness in each moment. You have the capacity.
- You can better your life by treating yourself with kindness and respect all the time.
- Choose to think positively about yourself and your life. It will uplift you.
- Stay conscious of loving yourself. Keep on it.

- If you misstep, just correct your course and keep going. Self-love is a journey and a state of being.
- You are perfect, even though nobody's perfect.
- Within you there is beauty.
- Your heart is a treasure.
- On the inside you are a radiant star. Affirm that.
- Inside your light sparkles. Be kind to your inner light.
- When you feel down, hug yourself. Really. Wrap your arms around yourself and squeeze. Pat your back like you would if you were hugging someone.
- Find the things that make your heart sing and do them.
- Say "I love myself" at least three times per day aloud or in your mind.
- Practice.

Only an emotionally healthy person is truly able to deal with their world in an emotionally healthy manner. *The Compassion Revolution* is in large part a quest to love and accept yourself so you can love and accept the rest of the world.

Seeking external validation brings disappointment.
Validate yourself from within to find true happiness.
#thecompassionrevolution

Day 21

Find Compassion Within through Your Own Spiritual Path

If only you could surpass your father in the investment world. If only you could show those jerks from college how far you've come. If only your ex could see what a happy marriage you have. So much vitriol is on the verge of combustion in the churning cauldron of our chaotic psyches. The "if onlys" are sometimes distant memories, and sometimes they bubble up. In that moment of bubble up, if you could let go, right then, you could cease the endless competition with the invisible father, schoolmate, or ex-girlfriend.

How relaxing it would be. How liberating to feel your own authentic motivations instead of your psyche's sometimes distorted influence over your actions. Next time you notice, with all of your new self-observation, that you are being influenced by a feeling of competition, choose to let go and relax your heart right then. Instead, choose self-compassion. Like a drum, start a new rhythm within you. Beat it strong and clear in your heart: *compassion*.

You are opening the door to a whole new world, one that is sought as a spiritual pinnacle by some. Except you are your own guru, and like the Dalai Lama has said, "This is my simple religion. There is no need for temples; no need for complicated philosophy. Our own brain, our own heart is our temple; the philosophy is kindness."

The central idea of most religions is to treat others the way you would like to be treated and to love one another. In many ways that is the essence of compassion. World religions have promoted compassion through the lighter and most inclusive parts of their teachings. And the energy and spirit that people feel when connecting through these philosophical and religious frameworks may perhaps be the result of feeling spirit, also known as interconnection, love, compassion, and light. What if light is all we need to cultivate compassion?

The more we take time to understand other cultures and religions, the more we can live from compassion. It's valuable to look at the different ways that compassion is highlighted in some of these older and contemporary teachings. At this time, the age of becoming your own guru, we can adopt the beliefs and practices that resonate with us and our value systems with ease and grace.

Buddhism is actually a philosophy, not a religion. It teaches that compassion is the answer to everything in life, from peace on earth to the peace of every family and even harmony among the animals. Buddhism teaches that compassion is the highest level of motivation and that all this suffering in life can be stopped by generating compassion for each other. Buddhism is a complex philosophy and goes far beyond doctrine, to the point that most adherents consider it a lifestyle and not a church. The Buddhist path involves living a moral life, becoming aware of the motivations behind thought and actions, and developing a deeper wisdom.

Modern **Druidism** was born of Celtic-era Druidry, which teaches harmony and worship of nature. This means having respect not only for one's neighbor, but also for the earth itself. In addition to worshipping nature, Druidry also includes the worship of ancestors. Druidry dates back to the ancient Celtic and Pagan religions, in which Druids operated as priests. Many Druids and Pagans believe in unconditional love, compassion, respect, forgiveness, and gratitude, as well as the five elements of spirit, water, air, fire, and earth. Nature supports all life through compassion, and it is a quality that is evident in all creation. Druids and Pagans even teach that spirit and compassion are so closely linked that as you grow more unconditionally compassionate, spirit will send more opportunities your way. Compassion ultimately lies in recognizing the kinship that exists between all living things and that we are all related to each other, not only as the same species but also sharing common ancestors in evolution.

Native American spiritual tradition and culture is multi-layered because of the many tribes and different belief systems that each one adopted. They range from monotheistic to polytheistic to animistic. Like Aboriginal Australians, the Native Americans didn't write these stories down but put more emphasis on oral histories, allegories, and teachers. Much of what Americans take for granted about the mediation legal process is derived from Native American law and standards of respect that their people had for each other. They taught mutual and cooperative respect for the points of view of others. For example, in one tradition, the "talking stick" allows the one holding it to speak, while the others have to listen without interrupting—a standard we adapted into courtroom procedure.

In **Judaism**, while the Torah may speak of God allowing Noah to eat animals, much of the later writings emphasize showing compassion to animals and not causing unnecessary pain. Ancient Jews always considered compassion a virtue, making it law to look after orphans, widows, and even strangers. Italian Jewish scholar Samuel David Luzatto said that having compassion is its own reward. Whereas many other faiths believe in some form of heaven, the Jews do not try to predict what the afterlife involves. Therefore, being compassionate is not done with expectations of making it to paradise. It is simply what they ought to do, because that's just the right thing to do.

Christianity is based upon the teachings of the Bible and specifically on the life and teachings of Jesus Christ, a man known for his compassionate attitude and his golden rule of "do unto others." To love your neighbor isn't enough, or so Jesus once said, because the real test of love is to forgive your enemies. Jesus did exactly that, praying for the very men who killed him, as recorded in the book of Luke. In the book of John he said, "A new command I give you: Love one another. As I have loved you, so you must love one another" (13:34).

Islam is a religion that has more in common with Judaism and Christianity than it has differences. Islam comes from the same Abrahamic lineage that started the two other big religions. Where it differs is in the role of Muhammad, whom Muslims consider to be the last prophet of God, following in the footsteps of Adam, Moses, Abraham, and Jesus Christ. Islam's greatest expansion was in the Golden Age of the Islamic Empire from 700 to 1200 CE, and the current population of 1.6 billion is quickly increasing. Every time a Muslim prays, he invokes the "peaceful names" of God, *Rahman* and *Rahim*, which mean "compassionate" and "merciful." So every time a Muslim addresses God, he begins with God's compassionate name and compassionate quality. Compassion is not necessarily suffering with others, as if suffering is a good thing, but means that one person is able to lessen the burden on another person. The opposite of compassion in Islam is to be apathetic to a person's pain. Sensitivity toward others is the ideal, as well as avoiding arrogant behavior.

I propose the idea that everyone is their own guru. As we continue as a society to let go of hierarchical dogma and structures, we will find that the meaning and spiritual energy that we are seeking outside of ourselves is actually within. It's been there all along. And it is the source of everything including compassion. Make compassion your religion to live a life of meaning and joy.

—— *Activity* ——
Find Divinity Within

You have the unique opportunity in modern times in the Western world to choose your own spiritual path. You may end up combining spiritual traditions from many different religions or philosophies. And you may choose to forge a brand new path.

I believe that we have entered the age where there are no more gurus because everyone has the opportunity to be their own guru. Yes, teachers abound. But what if the ultimate universal life force that courses through us all has the power to open the door to your own inner divine nature?

You are your own guru.

And you can put your focus on whatever brings you the most joy and fulfillment. Perhaps meditation expands your mind and heart in ways you never imagined. Perhaps the study of Kabbalah brings order to the world in a way that you've always craved. Perhaps the tenets of a certain Native American philosophy resonate with you deeply.

Whatever works for you is absolutely perfect.

So pull out your journal and a pen or some colored pencils and markers and answer the following questions. You can write your answers or even draw pictures of them.

1. What are some ways that you enjoy being creative? Creating art? Drawing, painting? Dancing? Singing? Writing or creating poetry? Woodworking? List three to five things that come to mind.

2. Next, what word do you like to use to describe the universal energy or life force that flows through us all? Do you like the word "God"? "Goddess"? "Great mystery"? "Divinity"? "Spirit"? "Source"? "The one"?

3. Is there anything about existing religions to which you've been exposed that does not resonate with you? You can make a brief note of that.

4. Do you prefer to connect with spiritual energy solo or in a group, or do you like both?

5. Do you feel like something is missing spiritually and you want to put more energy and attention on that part of your life?

Review your answers afterward and contemplate them. An ideal situation may be easily visible through this contemplation.

On the other hand, you may just need to sit with these answers for a time and see what emerges. But this is the first step of taking ownership of your own spiritual path.

Find the light within you through meditation and introspection,
and you will illuminate your life from within.
#thecompassionrevolution

Day 22

Witnessing Lack of Love and Staying Open

Today I am seeking understanding. This week there were two major terrorist attacks. And my heart hurts. I think many of us feel this way. The sadness over what is happening can be overwhelming. The suffering that's being created is seemingly needless, senseless, and maddening. We all feel so helpless. What can we really do? How can we help bring about an end to suffering? And why are these people, called terrorists, suffering so much? I go back to all the children who grow up to be these perpetrators of massive senseless violence—who were they? Why did they become this way? And I seek answers, but I don't know if there are any. So today I'm going to meditate with Tara and Kwan Yin, who are goddesses of compassion, and I'm going to share with you what I experience because maybe it can help all of us. I invite you to set aside time to meditate with Tara and Kwan Yin as well. And I hope that by the time you read this book these senseless, violent events have stopped. Today I'm praying for compassion to reign on earth.

Meditation with Tara

I decided to write a letter to the goddess of compassion, Tara, and then meditate and listen for answers. Here's what I wrote:

> *Dear Tara,*
>
> *I'm writing you today because I'm so confused by the duality of our world. I don't understand why suffering exists. And I know in spiritual teachings it usually just comes back to accepting it and doing your best to change it. Most of the time I can be satisfied with that, but I'm having a hard time about today. Please share your wisdom with me so I can better understand this reality.*
>
> *With love,*
> *Amy*

As I sat in meditation, I repeated the mantra *shanti*, which means "peace." Shanti. Shanti. Shanti. Next, I asked to connect with Tara directly, and I felt her presence in the room. My body got very hot, and I started sweating. I felt fiery, white heat pouring in through my crown chakra, at the top of my head. My hands began to pulse, and I felt this hot, intense energy flowing down from my head through my whole body and into the earth. Tara helped me get back in the flow. That is something I call "proper universal alignment." Those words can also be used like a mantra, repeated over and over to realign you with your life and your highest good: Proper universal alignment. Proper universal alignment. Proper universal alignment.

As I felt like I was sitting with Tara, we held hands—me with my physical hands and her with her spirit hands. Before me she had bright white light as her body and white garments flowed behind her, made of energy. The background behind her looked like space. I felt her in a deeper cosmic way than I had before. Although I've worked with her for many years with my medical intuitive clients, it is seldom that I come to her for help for myself. As she sat across from me, she sent a white, glowing light from her heart to mine, and I opened my heart as best as I could and accepted it. I let it flow when I repeated the word "yes" as a mantra. Yes, yes, yes.

In my meditation I learned that she understood that it is hard to witness lack of love, which is the cause of suffering. Lack is an illusion. It isn't real, and even though the experiences that we all have are real, the lack is like a bad dream or a hologram. It is a reality that we have the power to step out of even though we will continue to live in this world.

Tara told me she would never advise us to ignore suffering in the world and that we can all help. Each day we can spend ten minutes meditating for peace and compassion. Each day we can spread love in this world through our actions, thoughts, and words, and each day we can endeavor to accept the shadow self within us. All of the discord and suffering in the world is a mirror of the discord and suffering within the human race.

The best thing we can do to help prevent future world tragedies is dive deep within our beings and integrate every single shadow part of ourselves that is in existence. If everyone on earth did this, all of the external manifestations of disturbance and discord would cease. The human race is like one giant family. We have all made an agreement to be here in this rotating tapestry of souls and to slowly, like sand through a sifter, sift out the shadow parts and eventually emerge like a phoenix with crystals of light. We are all engaging in this process whether we do it consciously or unconsciously, but it is a lot easier and causes a lot less suffering if we do it consciously.

As I felt Tara step back, I was still filled with the vision of bright white light. Below I will share the gist of the process to integrate the shadow.

Integrate Your Shadow Self

Your "shadow" self is the part of you that stays hidden away for nobody to see. Occasionally, you might catch a glimpse of it, in a moment of partially suppressed rage or stark loneliness. The shadow is a very personal aspect of the total self. It is everything you find unpalatable, unattractive, or socially unacceptable that is a part of you no matter how deeply it is buried within. Your shadow can be scary, for it contains all that you fear, especially about yourself. Your inner malice, manipulations, jealousy, envy, and madness. It's the sad little child hiding in the corner after being rejected, and it's the bully on the playground who terrorizes others. It's the power-hungry monster within, and it's the helpless supplicant victim. Your shadow is everything you can't control. Your very own personal inner chaos.

When we bury or repress aspects of ourselves, they will manifest or "act out" like wayward children. This can occur on many levels. Our shadows can manifest in the form of other people who wrong us; they hold up a mirror to help us more clearly see ourselves. Our deeply buried shadows can color and influence situations in our lives and manifest situations that mirror all aspects of the self.

Global and societal events through the ages have held up a mirror to humanity, to our collective shadow as a race and as a planet. Our shadow selves have played a part in many world events through the ages. As beings gaining cosmic consciousness at a critical time in the planet's evolution, an opportunity exists to take responsibility for our shadows. This means integrating our own personal shadows, to the best of our abilities, to make less energy available for manifestations of darkness. In the constant movement toward balance, if there is less repressed shadow energy being held by the beings of the earth, then there is less of a need for events and situations that we cannot ignore, to make us stand and take notice of our shadows. Doing this integrative work raises vibration on an individual level and raises the vibration of the planet.

Welcoming Your Shadow Back Meditation

Use this process to integrate your own shadow only. This is individual work that is best done consciously; do not do this for others. Everyone must take responsibility for their own shadow side.

Go within and into your heart space. See yourself standing in a temple in the center of your heart chamber. Notice the surroundings and walk over to the altar in the center of the temple. If it is bare, cover it with things that bring you joy, like flowers, tropical fruits, minerals, pictures, artwork, statues of deities, or songs.

Then stand tall, proud, and strong. Raise your spirit arms above your head in the temple as you stand physically at home or out in nature and do the same.

Speak the following out loud with clarity of intention: "I call all aspects of myself to the center of my heart chamber. All are welcome in the temple. You will be received with love. My shadow, hear my call. It is time to integrate."

See your shadow stand before you in the center of your heart temple. Do not judge it. Look it straight in the eye. Know it. Feel white light or love emanate from your spirit self, from your hands and heart and eyes. Love your shadow. Allow balance to enter your soul structure and permeate your being. Offer your shadow a home in your heart temple. Perceive the wholeness that stems from shadow integration. Feel the oneness in welcoming all that you are into the center of the temple of your heart.

Use this process as often as you would like. Know that you have made a difference in the world with the responsibility you took and the light you magnetized.

Meditation with Kwan Yin, Goddess of Compassion

Next let's meditate with Kwan Yin, the goddess of compassion, who was also known as Avalokiteshvara in Buddhist philosophy. As noted earlier, Buddhism is not a religion. It's a philosophy. It's simply a way of viewing the world. It does not have gods or a creator. At the philosophy's core the idea is that mindfulness, being present, and meditation can increase people's quality of life. A wonderful book that gives an impartial history and explanation of Buddhism is called *A Little Bit of Buddha*. I also recommend a book called *The Untethered Soul* that aids in meditation and nonattachment.

As a medical intuitive, I have been acquainted with the being known as Kwan Yin for many years. She has provided me with solace, comfort, and insights, as well as lots of healing for my clients. So it's always an honor and a joy to communicate with her.

I sat down to meditate with her and asked her to sit with me and guide me in cultivating more compassion and understanding how to bring compassion to my life and how to view our world through a compassionate lens. She shared some wisdom with me through automatic writing, which is similar to channeling but done through a written medium instead of spoken.

During my meditation, Kwan Yin told me it is valuable to center yourself in the idea of compassion to bring forward new energy from your core. Your core is a powerful, generating dynamo. It is where everything inside of you springs forth from. And what is within you creates your external world. Your core, energy, and personality interact with this world and create what some people call karma, which is really simply energy. This energy or karma then causes a type of celestial weather within you. It interacts with the pure light of your inner core and creates a variety of conditions in your body and being. You can control this to a certain degree with your mind and your thoughts. You can also try to cultivate certain emotions and feelings and influence the neutral energy that comes from your core-spring in the directions that you choose. Sometimes, though, life happens and bumps against your energy and shifts things. But you have the power to become conscious of when that happens and shift it back or in whatever direction you would like. You hold the ultimate power.

Kwan Yin told me that a wonderful way to become more self-aware that lets you know how you're directing your energy is meditation. Meditation is a process of letting your mind relax and take whatever time it needs to calm down and cease its chatter. Then you enter into the witnessing self, the part of you that is simply present. It is the part of you that is inside of you looking out and watching you have the experiences that you have each day. The witnessing self doesn't really act; it just watches.

Look at this book and see yourself reading the words. Who is inside watching you read these words? That is your witnessing self. When you meditate, you allow the mind to slow down its chatter, as much as you can, and then you begin to become more and more aware of the witnessing self. The witnessing self never gets its feathers ruffled. It doesn't have a lot of desires. It just watches. It's very calm and peaceful. It's also very compassionate. It's not attached, but it does care. The more you can be in your witnessing self, the more you can find peace within and the more you can be in compassion.

—— *Activity* ——
Connect with Kwan Yin

To rest in your witnessing self, take a few moments and sit or lie down quietly. When you're ready, close your eyes and breathe deeply. Notice what's happening in your mind. Just let yourself begin to slow down. Next, you can use a mantra to focus your attention on one word. That way the rest of the mind's chatter can wind down. Sometimes this takes a while. It can also take practice, and it's not something that you're ever going to get a grade on or win at; it's something you do for you.

You can choose any words you would like as a mantra. Here are some suggestions: "compassion," "peace," "love," "joy," "yes," and "tranquility." Calm and quiet the mind, follow your breathing, and then begin to repeat your mantra. Do this for as long as you'd like. Notice what the witnessing self is up to. Notice it watching as you repeat the mantra. Pay attention to how your thoughts are slowing down.

Now, if you would like, you can connect with Kwan Yin during your meditation. To do this, simply say aloud or in your mind, "I now connect with Kwan Yin, goddess of compassion, for my highest good and the highest good of all life."

She is sitting before you. Reach out your hands and place them palms up in front of you. Nod your head to let her know that it is okay for her to hover her spirit hands over your hands. As you feel her hands hovering over yours, feel the connection between you being made. You may feel a pulsing of energy. You may feel tingling, a cold or hot sensation in your palms, or a feeling or a sense of serenity, or you may even smell a particular smell. You may see certain colors or get certain feelings in your body.

You can now say hello to Kwan Yin. Thank her for connecting with you, and pause to let her say hello back. If you have anything that you would like help with, you can now ask her. You can sit quietly in meditation with your hands connected with hers and allow yourself to receive any answers or energy that can help you with whatever you've asked about. If you'd like, you can ask her if she would like any help with anything from you and let her know that you are available to help her with her work for the highest good. When that feels complete, the energy between your hands will begin to slow down and stop, and you'll just naturally bring your hands back to your sides. Then thank her out loud if you can and state aloud, "I now disconnect with Kwan Yin, as needed, for my highest good." Feel her presence gently recede but know that she is near and always available. You can connect with her this way as much as you would like.

I allow the deities of compassion
to fill me with light for the highest good.
#bethelight #thecompassionrevolution

Day 23

The Interconnection Mindset

Open your mind to this idea: we are all the same being. Imagine that every soul is actually the same—one soul, one energy—differentiated into infinite universes in an endless existence. I believe this is the reality of existence. You will hear lots of things in New Age circles about karma and reincarnation and the reality of life. The amazing thing about the great mystery of existence is in some ways we will never completely know these answers while we are here on earth. I will share with you my perspective gleaned from being clairvoyant for as long as I can remember and pursuing the truth of our reality for my entire life. As a medical intuitive for the last fifteen years, I have had the amazing opportunity of witnessing thousands of people's myriad varieties of incarnation. That means everything from helping people clear their karma to talking to their deceased relatives and even learning about the transition process of their pets and friends. What I've gleaned from all these years learning about soul and spirit from thousands of people is that existence is mind-bendingly complicated and at the same time paradoxically simple. The bottom line is we are all one. We are all the same being.

The energy of interconnection permeates everything we do and experience and every moment of our lives. Even as I write this book, I am interconnected with all of the items in my office, my desk, the tree outside the window, the other people in the neighborhood, the plants and animals surrounding me, and the entire world. When I tap into that interconnection, I feel it throughout my body but especially in my heart. The center of the chest that is known as the heart chakra is a top place where we are able to palpably sense and feel the energy of love in our physical bodies. The natural extension of the feelings of interconnection is the feeling of love. When we really home in on what love actually is, we understand that it is spirit. It is what some people called divinity. It is also compassion, caring, and the embracing feeling of connection and interconnection that is possible. Divine love flows through all of us. It is energy, pure and simple. Energy itself can be neutral and given a flavor. When we apply this flavor of love to energy, we connect with many of the things that we consider pleasant in life. Interconnection is really love.

I have always had a strong connection with whales and dolphins. And I have had many amazing synchronistic experiences that have allowed me to swim with them in the wild. These experiences are amazing gifts and blessings in my life that I am eternally grateful for. For example, the experience of swimming with humpback whales in the wild several times through what appeared to be incredible coincidence changed my life. I'd like to share a message that I received from whales about interconnection in 2009. I have been doing automatic writing for the past twenty years, and that is how this information was shared.

Message from the Finback Whales

Imagine what the gentle giants known as finback whales might say about interconnection. Here is what I imagine:

> *Dear greetings, gentle ones.*
>
> *We enjoy your human energy in many ways. We sense so many of you yearning for growth and change. You feel our planet is a profound resource now. This is good. It is moving you toward seeing the radiant beauty of the entirety of your existence as a race and of you as an individual.*
>
> *Our planet is so amazingly beautiful! We share this planet, you and us. We are one—a united state of interconnection. One world. Interconnected. United earth—one global matrix of light.*
>
> *This is our essence, interconnection. You can avail yourself of our matrix and feel the beauty that exists here. We are aware of our innate connection with all existence in each moment of our lives. Even as babies we are intercon-*

nected and feel it. We can feel each of the planet's insects, blades of grass, and emotions deeply and richly at all times. We are the ultimate empaths.

We sometimes keep to ourselves because our multidimensional lives are so rich. Our lives are full of interconnected heart love and deep peace. We are sensitive beings, and we require peace and silence.

Imagine the deep quiet of the deeper waters. Imagine yourself immersed there.

Resting.

Feel why we are so connected: because our peace is deep. We take time for ourselves as individuals, and yet we love the peaceful stability of our species' society. We all know each other well because of this interconnection. So it is. Love and peace to you.

Love,
Your Finback Friends

—— *Activity* ——
I Matter, You Matter, We Matter

If I had only one mission with this book, it would be to communicate clearly and unequivocally to every reader that you matter. You matter. Really take that in. Do you think you matter? Do you think that your existence makes any difference in anything? In your heart, do you feel like you matter? A lot of people would say no. Many of us don't believe that we matter. Many of us don't connect with the fact that everything we do affects the world around us.

On any given day as you walk out of your apartment and up the street to the nearest store, you create ripples of energy. Your thoughts, your feelings, how you carry yourself, what you do, and what you don't do all affect the world around you.

When you walk into the store to get your supplies—let's say you even go to the self-checkout line—you are still going to encounter people and in those moments affect those people's lives. A single moment can change a life permanently. Sometimes that can be for the better.

Here's an example: Let's imagine a person who only goes out of his house one day a month. It's likely he's depressed or agoraphobic or maybe both. So on that walk to the store up the street, this man passes a mother and daughter. The daughter is around six. The daughter looks at him with curiosity and smiles at him as they pass. He smiles back involuntarily. The man is dressed in ratty clothing. He doesn't look upscale or pleasant like most of the people this young girl sees on a day-to-day basis because she goes to private school and lives a more upscale life. After the man has gone to the store and comes back out, he is heading back up the street to his apartment. Coming the other way are the mother and daughter finishing whatever errand they did at the other end of the street. Before they pass each other, the paper on the bottom of the man's grocery bag gives way, and his groceries fall to the ground. The mother holds the daughter's hand and tries to pull her past, but the daughter turns, stops, and goes to try to help the man. At first the mother tries to pull her away, but then she too begins to notice what is going on around her and helps as well. She pulls one of her reusable shopping bags out of her purse and helps him put his groceries in it. They all end up talking and eventually go on their way.

Of course, we'd like to hold that the positive experiences the man had with people would inspire him to leave his apartment more. But the thing that might have happened in this situation is that the mother was pulled back into noticing other people and out of her own reverie of busyness. And the daughter had the opportunity to connect with someone who didn't look like everyone else in her world. She had the opportunity to see something different and as a result lay the groundwork for compassion and empathy. All of this resulted from one day a super isolated man had to leave his apartment to get groceries. He mattered. He didn't try to matter. He certainly wasn't looking to matter in anyone's life. But he did, nonetheless. We never know how small moments might shape lives. It could be that that moment planted the seed that inspired that six-year-old girl to go to college and choose a profession that helps others.

Activity —
Creative Compassion

Now we are going to do a creative activity. If you have a journal, take it out. I'd like you to create a story. In this story you matter, and people in your world matter. This can be as practical or whimsical as you choose. In this activity we create a fictional story because it gives your mind and heart free reign to work out any inner conflicts you might have about the idea of compassion. It also gives you the opportunity to think big and get really creative about how a fictional character could enact more compassion. It doesn't put pressure on you that you have to do it all today; it just opens a door in our mind to the possibility of someone somewhere enacting your story. This level of creative expression is one where innovation and extraordinary thoughts happen. Let this activity be a fun way to express your creativity around a poignant topic like compassion.

Your story could be that you go to the gym, talk to someone in the locker room, and pay them a compliment, and it is the shared smile between you that turns that person's day around and makes it better. Or it can be something far-fetched, like you are transplanted into the world of Star Wars. You are on Kashyyyk, the planet from which Chewbacca hails, and you help deliver a Wookiee baby who later grows up to help the Rebels and his uncle Chewie defeat the First Order. (Yes, I'm a Star Wars nerd.)

Sit down with your journal and set a timer for fifteen minutes. Outline the concept of your story and then start filling it in. It can just be a page long; it doesn't have to be too extensive if you do not want to make it that way. The purpose of this activity is to help you home in on all of the types of situations in which you make a difference. Because the truth is that every second of every day you are making a difference. Everything you do affects somebody, even if it's just you. The choice to meditate before bed or not may influence how short your temper is later in the week and whether or not you yell at your children or choose gentler communication. Every choice does matter. You matter. And so does everyone else on this planet. The person who is standing at a stoplight holding a sign asking for money and who could be on drugs or a scam artist or really in need matters too. Even just standing there with the sign is going to inspire all kinds of different feelings in everyone who drives by, from guilt for not helping to anger at them for not doing an honest day's work if someone is feeling judgmental. And everything else you can think of. You may or may not decide to help them or give the money, but know that they do matter. When so many humans on this planet are suffering so much, it affects all of us. Instead of getting depressed and feeling overwhelmed and helpless, we can all choose to make small positive differences every day. So write a story about that. Let your imagination have free reign to open your mind to the possibilities that compassion brings.

Everything you do matters.
Every time you share and care, the light multiplies.
#thecompassionrevolution

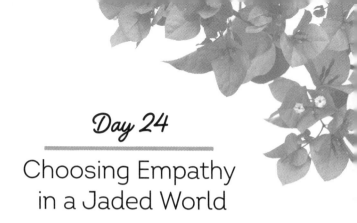

Day 24

Choosing Empathy in a Jaded World

Yesterday, I was getting adjusted by my chiropractor, who is also a dear friend, and I asked her a question. I said, "Do you think back in time that early humans experienced subluxation and the discomfort that it causes so many of us? Do you think because they were running around so much and not sitting or standing at desks, their spines naturally stayed aligned?" (Subluxation is a slight misalignment of the vertebrae.)

She said, "I think that they were more externally focused, and so it didn't affect them." Her answer was really profound when you think about it. People were running around, potentially in handmade clothing and potentially in bare feet, and hunting and gathering in a wide variety of climates—hot and cold, rain and snow and ice. Their comfort level was probably low. And they didn't notice that their back hurt or their neck hurt or whatever else because they were so externally focused. Because they were worried about the next animal that would attack their camp, the next neighboring tribe that would cause problems, the next torrential rain or snowstorm, or how to find enough food and water. Their lives were focused on their external world because it dictated their survival.

Nowadays, in many instances around the world we have removed the question of immediate survival. Although people may be worried about money and the economy, many know it's likely that they'll have food to eat tomorrow. They know it's pretty likely that they will sleep in their own bed tonight under a toasty comforter with the heat on. These questions of immediate survival have been largely removed. Because of this, we have the opportunity to look within. And we've begun this process. Even harking back to the troubadours in the Middle Ages, some of the questions of immediate survival were answered, and people began to prize creativity and enjoy stories of romance and fairy tales. They were seeking mental and emotional stimulation and enjoyment.

Fast forward to now, and as a species we have been pondering our internal world for years. We notice now if our wrist hurts from typing. We notice if in our softball game last night we might have misaligned our shoulder, and we take steps to remedy the situation. We purchase ice packs to strap on our wrist. We consult a chiropractor or health practitioner to realign our shoulder or spine. We've learned that introspection and self-awareness can identify problems or discomforts. And from that we've extrapolated that we have the power to take action to alleviate portions of our discomfort.

The thing that I think is amazing about this is that as we tune into things that are not how we want them to be and take action, we increase our awareness of our internal experience. And a lot of us spend a good portion of our lives this way now. I believe that the next evolutionary step in consciousness will result as we become excruciatingly self-aware of every unpleasant feeling, thought, and bodily sensation. The next natural step will be to begin to pass that kind of idea on to other people. We will begin to ask ourselves, does this unpadded seat affect the person next to me the way it affected me by bothering my tailbone? We've already started down that path! One where we provide caring and empathy for others. But I believe this is just the beginning! As humans in the Western world bore of trying to solve their endless list of problems and complaints, I believe many will increasingly seek spiritual answers to life's questions. Through that process, people will even more consciously begin to care about and think about others. This all-encompassing level of self-awareness that some of us feel is the precursor to expanded consciousness. It's the precursor to the next evolutionary step of compassion in action because we will begin to care about other people's small discomforts as well. This can give us an opportunity to work as a team to alleviate the small discomforts faced by many and with each step move closer to an end to suffering on our planet.

Think about where you are in that process. For me, as a highly sensitive person, every little bodily sensation, every tweak of the neck when I lift a weight the wrong way feels like a cataclysm in my body. And I know that I have all of the health markers that indicate a lower tolerance for pain—thin cell walls in the brain that with a certain kind of magnesium deficiency lead to migraine headaches. I'm also clairvoyant and intuitive with most of my senses, so that means I'm sensitive to everything. I've learned how to manage it. But, yes, small things affect me more than other people, and I can say from personal experience that as a result I am extremely aware of small things that affect other people. I will offer people cushions to sit on. I will ask friends how certain life events are affecting them emotionally. Because I'm sensitive, I see more and sense more, and it has made me an extremely empathetic and compassionate person.

I believe that we all have infinite capability to be sensitive, empathic, clairvoyant, psychic—all of it. Some of us are born that way, just like some people are born with musical talent. But everyone can learn to play a musical instrument whether or not they're born with that talent fully expressed. It's the same thing with intuition and empathy: everyone can learn to be intuitive. And absolutely everyone has the capability to be empathic. It just takes practice.

Empathy is defined as the ability to understand the feelings of another person or being. And when we can put ourselves in someone else's shoes, real compassion can be the result. I believe this is the direction that our society is headed. Don't be discouraged by what you see in the media. Nowadays it is their job to show you the most fear-inducing, intense, and dramatic things possible to get your adrenaline pumping and engage the frontal lobe of your brain so that you watch more and in that heightened state might buy more. But the truth is, in spite of all the things that the media tells you to the contrary, the world is becoming a better place every day. We are evolving. Many things are wrong, absolutely. And we can try our best to change what we can. But we are all growing in our compassion and empathy toward one another, and eventually this will extend more and more to people in other countries and all around the world. We can help this process along by cultivating compassion within ourselves, modeling compassion and sensitivity to others, and sharing our light and caring with the world around us.

—— *Activity* ——
Risking Rejection to Help

As the light of compassion emerges within our souls, we begin to feel a call to do more. To help more people. To spread more light. It can be simple things, like kind words spoken, or larger things, like time spent volunteering. With this call to care echoing within us, we are gently forced into potentially more uncomfortable situations. Because sometimes when we try to help, we will get rejected.

Rejection is a part of life. We experience that when we apply for a job that we don't get. In my life I experience it when publishers don't always buy what I'm selling. In your life you might even experience it with friends or family or your spouse. Little experiences of rejection are like dog training for us. They teach us that we do not get a hit of dopamine or any other feel-good chemical when we're rejected, and so we're discouraged to enact that behavior again.

We have to rally against our training to avoid rejection. Instead, we need to cultivate an attitude of nonattachment. With this attitude, we are happy to offer any help to anyone that does not diminish us or our vital life force in any way, but we are not attached to whether they accept it. Sometimes we tend to take it personally if someone doesn't accept our offer of kindness or help. We need to untrain ourselves to react this way and retrain ourselves to frequently, easily, and authentically share our love and caring with compassion like it is as easy as breathing. And we need to encourage ease with that process so that we feel good whether or not our help is received and it does not diminish the likelihood that we will offer it again.

Try to think for a minute about situations in which you have offered to help somebody out of empathy and have been rejected. Use these opportunities for contemplation to increase your self-awareness. Instead of getting offended, ask yourself what you could have done differently. How could you reframe the experience for yourself so that it would be positive?

Today, I challenge you to commit to offering compassionate assistance to someone in the next twenty-four hours. But I want you to do this with no expectation of praise, gratitude, reward, or even acknowledgment. And no attachment to whether or not the person actually accepts the help. I know that is a tall order. I'm giving you a real challenge! But I know you can do it.

The idea of nonattachment or detachment simply means releasing our attachments to a certain outcome, a certain reaction from someone, or any desire for physical things, emotional states, or world situations. Many religions and philosophies talk about this concept, including Buddhism, Christianity, the Bahá'í Faith, Taoism, Hinduism, and Islam. It is also popular in twelve-step programs like Alcoholics Anonymous, Alateen, and Al-Anon. People who study a course in miracles also familiarize themselves with this concept of nonattachment.

Nonattachment has become a spiritual idea in our society. Perhaps it is. But it is also a psychologically healthy mindset. It is the opposite of what some people call codependence. And it is a great way to not be attached to specific things that you desire on this earthly plane. When you combine nonattachment with all-encompassing compassion and love, you have attained a higher perspective. This is something we can all aim for and try to create within ourselves. Everyone makes mistakes, and we won't always do everything perfectly. We can cultivate an attitude of not being attached to specific outcomes but instead have an empathic and compassionate view of the world and make the choice to take action to help those around us while also extending the utmost kindness and compassion to ourselves.

So this is the mindset I want you to be in when you do your next compassionate act in the twenty-four hours following reading this. See if you can be gently nonattached and lovingly empathic while being sure to vigorously care for yourself.

It is a trifecta of self-awareness, consciousness, and awareness of your world. Rise to the challenge today!

Let go of rejections and focus on self-reflection. For it is within that you will find the light you seek.
#thecompassionrevolution

Day 25

Ending Bullying and Teaching Children Compassion

Before my career as a writer and during part of my career as a medical intuitive, I worked as a teacher for eight years. My college degree is in education. I spent a good part of the late '90s and early 2000s teaching children to care for one another and our world. I always made it a point to design activities based around altruism and empathy. I think these are essential qualities to teach children from an early age. Children need to understand that here in the Western world we're extremely privileged. Although we don't want to create any fear in children, we do want them to understand that there are people who could use our caring, and it is part of our job and privilege to be able to share it. I did small things like have a world flag in our classroom and talk about other countries and cultures. I also taught meditation in the classroom, which was effective at calming restless minds and bodies and getting everyone in the classroom ready for learning time. At the time, I didn't call it meditation, just quiet time, and I frequently led the children through a standard but abbreviated mindfulness practice. They learned to notice their breathing, think about the earth beneath them, and relax their bodies at will.

Meditating with Children

A popular quote attributed to the Dalai Lama that has gone viral on the Internet asserts, "If every eight-year-old in the world is taught meditation, we will eliminate violence from the world within one generation." Although this may sound simplistic and idealistic, it certainly contains a kernel of truth.

The effects of meditation on learning and cognition with children are astounding. In my work as a kindergarten teacher, the days we meditated in a circle for a few minutes in the morning ensured we had a much smoother day. Adele Diamond and Kathleen Lee wrote in a 2011 study in the journal *Science*, "After mindfulness training, greater EF [executive function] improvements were found in 7–9 year-olds with initially-poorer EFs than those with initially-better EFs, compared with controls (who silently read). Children with initially poor EFs showed EF improvements overall and in the components of shifting and monitoring, bringing their scores up to average. Both teachers and parents reported these improvements, suggesting they generalized across contexts. The mindfulness training sessions consisted of three parts: sitting meditation;

activities to promote sensory awareness, attention regulation, or awareness of others or the environment; and a body scan."

Executive functions are defined in this study as creativity, flexibility, self-control, discipline, and "the cognitive control functions needed when you have to concentrate and think, when acting on your initial impulse would be ill-advised.... Core EFs are cognitive flexibility, inhibition (self-control, self-regulation), and working memory. More complex EFs include problem-solving, reasoning, and planning." This type of training on a cognitive level helps children think through actions before taking them. One application for this training is in the consideration of conflict. Before instigating a physical fight, a child might think the process through and develop a creative alternative to fighting.

These types of small actions in childhood result in adults who promote peace in their worlds. Imagine the result of meditation practice for children with difficult home lives. It offers them an opportunity for solace within themselves and a tool for self-soothing and calming. And it is indeed a skill that can be practiced, and proficiency can be gained. As a teacher, I observed that children who practiced the mindfulness skills in the classroom were more likely to sustain appropriate behavior throughout the entire school day, and they were more likely to exhibit impulse control on the playground.

Appropriate behavior on the playground translates into appropriate behavior in high school, which translates into appropriate behavior in society as a conscious adult contributing beneficially to society. Not to mention that the skills for success in this world, such as creativity, flexibility, and self-control, are enhanced through meditation. These are the same skills that help us create a positive life. They help us understand how to take creative action in our lives to make things better. Development of these executive functions contributes to our ability to exhibit self-control when we know something is not the best for us, like watching ten hours of TV on our days off, eating poorly, or not exercising.

And the idea of being flexible adults in mind, heart, and spirit is a powerful one. Being flexible means you can roll with the punches of life. Because there will be punches. There will be ups and there will be downs. But when you are able to be flexible, you're less likely to exhibit and experience an extreme stress response when your boss moves up a deadline or the vendor for your business gets sick and can't deliver. You're flexible and creative, so you find a solution that will work.

Teaching children meditation is probably one of the single most long-lasting gifts you could give. The Dalai Lama mentions the age of eight. In my experience as an educator of children ages three to six, they all benefit from mindfulness meditation practice. They love tuning in to their environment, their bodies, and how they are feeling. It usually comes easily for them, and it's a useful skill to cultivate in order to give children the tools they need to succeed in life and be compassionate citizens of the world.

Many people also assert that meditation is a great remedy for ADHD and learning-disabled children. I definitely saw that as a teacher. And as an adult with ADHD and numerous learning disabilities, I can personally attest that experience with meditation vastly improved these conditions.

There are numerous resources available about teaching children meditation. Please check them out. Here is a quick outline of what I used to do with children in preschool and kindergarten, and it is appropriate for any age: I would have the children sit cross-legged and show them a few different ways to comfortably place their hands either in their lap, on their knees, or in the traditional meditation position with thumb and pointer finger pressed together. Most children usually choose the meditation position because it's comfortable and natural.

Next, I would instruct them to notice the feeling of the air as they take a breath in and blow breath out, to notice what it feels like, and to notice how it feels as it moves through their mouth and down into their lungs and their belly. Sometimes I would have them do that ten times. They take ten big breaths and feel it whooshing in and out of their mouths and down into their bellies. I would ask them to envision clouds in the sky just passing by when they started to think about something—just to watch the nearest cloud flow through on a gentle breeze and feel that thought drift away. I would usually tell them this is the time they can let their thoughts slow down and relax, but their minds feel happy and aware.

Meditation can be that simple! So if you have children of your own or children in your life that you care for, this is an activity you can do together that benefits you both. If you are meditating with children, you can also more formally introduce the concept of a mantra, a word or set of words that you repeat over and over to bring your focus back from your thoughts running away from you. A great mantra to use with children is "love." I also like the mantra "joy." You can learn more about joy-focused meditation in my book *Joyful Living: 101 Ways to Transform Your Spirit and Revitalize Your Life.*

The Epidemic of Bullying

According to DoSomething.org, 90 percent of fourth through eighth graders have experienced bullying, and over 3.2 million students have been subjected to bullying. There are numerous helpful references you can find for the practical ways to deal with bullying. The reason I'm bringing up the epidemic of bullying in a book about compassion is that we have an opportunity as parents, educators, and caretakers to sow the seeds of compassion early in children to help prevent and hopefully ultimately eradicate the epidemic of bullying that is growing in our schools. And don't think this problem is exclusive to children. Adults are bullied every day, and workplace bullying is becoming an increasingly common problem.

So, let's use our new knowledge of empathy and compassion and try to reason through this whole bullying epidemic. On my YouTube show *Fresh Talk with Amy Leigh Mercree*, I have an episode titled "#BullyingNoWay—Facts, Bystander Behavior, and How to Help," in which I interview community educator and victim advocate Christine Kobie. Christine shared so much wonderful knowledge with us during that episode that I wanted to use that information to reason through compassionate action to stop bullying. In the episode, she told us that bullying is any kind of ongoing behavior that is designed to put another person down or make them feel less than others. It is typically teasing and sometimes physical violence, and it often includes picking on someone, embarrassing them, tripping them, spreading rumors, taking their things, and behavior designed to get a rise out of someone. What Christine highlighted for us is that basically bullying is abuse. Whether physical, mental, emotional, or even spiritual, it is an act of violence.

The first question is, why would someone bully another person? What do they get out of it? To put this question in perspective, Christine shared a statistic from the website stopbullying .gov and told us that during the middle school years, 30 percent of children have been bullies. They have enacted behaviors that abuse other people. She told us that when she goes to schools to educate children, they talk about how bullying is always done in front of other people. It is seldom enacted one-on-one. She noticed that the common denominator is bullies trying to get increased attention from the students around them. Bullying behaviors provide a sense of power for the abuser over the victim. They feel more in control in that moment because they're controlling the situation, and if they are the ones doing the bullying, they will not get bullied. She said another key reason is that they are experiencing bullying somewhere else in their lives. This could be at home with parents or siblings or in another setting with peers. In that scenario, the child or bully has the opportunity to gain some of their power back, and they choose a bullying behavior to do that, simply because that is what they've learned. Christine explained that bullying is typically a learned behavior. You can bet a bully has been bullied somewhere else prior. You can see this is a cycle that could be never-ending, and it requires serious compassionate intervention to stop it.

We can use our empathic and compassionate senses and certainly try to always teach children (and ourselves, for that matter) to walk a mile in another's shoes. If we see someone being bullied in public or in our workplace, we have the power to take compassionate action, and we can teach children this as well. Christine shared that 70 percent of students have witnessed bullying. It is important to equip all children with skills that they can use to intervene nonviolently to help one another.

And this also might increase the likelihood that someone else helps them when the tables are turned.

Christine shared with us an amazing statistic: for over half the students who witnessed bullying and intervened in some way, the bullying behavior stopped within ten seconds! That is a wonderful statistic to share with children in your life. It shows us that we can be a part of changing bullying in our schools and that children are empowered to help one another. And it's extremely effective!

Bystander behavior is critical in stopping bullying. Instead of encouraging the bullying or laughing when bullying happens around them, if children are taught to be compassionate and intervene using the proven bystander behavior steps, their school culture can change. Some of the things to say that you can share with children in your life are simple, like "Hey, that's not cool" or "I think that's bullying. You should stop." Or say to the child being bullied, "I'm sorry that this person is being mean to you or disrespecting you."

Let's talk about the three D's of bystander behavior. These are great things that you can teach the children in your life and even share with your child's teachers if they're not aware. This is called active bystandership. Instead of passively sitting by, we take action to intervene and elevate the situation.

1. *Direct:* Interrupt the bullying situation either using words or by physically standing next to the victim.

Instruct kids to say things like, "That's not funny!" They can look disapprovingly at the bully and make sure not to laugh or join in. They can also talk to the person being bullied and tell them that they're sorry that it's happening as well as acknowledge that it's not okay.

2. *Distract:* Sometimes kids might be uncomfortable directly intervening. They might be afraid of getting bullied too. Or of people thinking that they are not cool. So they can instead use this strategy to distract the people involved. They can pay the victim a compliment, saying that they like their backpack. They can ask a totally unrelated question, like "What time is soccer practice?" They can tell either the bully or the victim that someone is looking for them in the cafeteria. This is a great strategy to defuse a difficult situation without making the bystander feel vulnerable.

3. *Delegate:* This simply means getting other people involved. It might be the bystander asking a friend who is across the hall to come over and distract everybody involved. It might be going to find a teacher or an adult to intervene. If it's a serious situation, it might even be calling 911. When bystanders delegate and get help, they also feel less vulnerable.

One of the reasons I think that people can be hesitant to interrupt a bullying situation is that they don't want to draw the fire of the bully toward themselves. They feel vulnerable or exposed. They're afraid. And that is okay. Of course in a perfect world we would all feel courageous and brave all of the time and stand up for what's right at every turn. And certainly we can aspire to that. But with bullying there are other alternatives. There are other ways to stop a situation. You can distract and delegate to defuse a tough situation. These are the types of things you can teach children early so that they know what to do when they encounter these problems later in life. Because according to Christine, 70 percent of them will.

The next thing to do is to later take the time to sympathize with the person who was bullied. That would mean to seek them out and tell them, "Hey, that was really rough earlier today, and I just want you to know that I support you." And the child or an adult would do this out of compassion and empathy. It's usually born out of the realization that that person experiencing the adversity could've been you, which takes us back to teaching children to imagine what it's like to walk a mile in someone else's shoes and to do to others what they would want done to them.

What are the spiritual implications of this epidemic? It seems to me that we have children and adults feeling increasingly inferior and needing outlets to bolster their sense of self. And these outlets are false outlets; people do not have the skill of seeking constructive and healthy ways to improve their self-esteem. We can blame it on lots of things, from the media to poor parenting to societal attitudes about gender, sexual orientation, race, or religion. But the underlying truth is we are experiencing lack of love in our society, lack of compassion, and lack of love for ourselves.

A question to ask yourself and any children in your life that you're discussing this topic with is this: Do you think bullies love themselves? We can guess the answer is likely no. We know they have probably been bullied before. We know that they're seeking power because they feel disempowered. We know that they feel like they are lacking in control in their lives. So, in essence, these people are in pain. And they're causing pain. This is how suffering is perpetuated in our society; pain begets more pain.

But we have the power to take a stand to choose love. To choose compassion. To teach empathy and caring to the children in our lives. To be idealists and envision a better world and take action to create it. Educate yourselves, the children in your life, and the teachers that you know, and hopefully we can all work together to create a better world, free of bullying, where everyone feels loved and empowered and doesn't feel the need to diminish another. This bumpy road we are on is leading our planet to consciousness. How long will it take? I have no idea. But I think if we work together to raise compassion and consciousness, we can shorten the journey.

My Personal Story of Experiencing Bullying in Middle School

In middle school, I was still growing into myself. I had a really round face, a super curly perm with short hair, gangly and long arms and legs, and a round midsection. If I knew my younger self now, I would say I was a normal, young teenager. But back then I felt like an overweight pumpkin head. I had acne and braces—the whole nine yards.

I can remember a particular week when I had gotten a new pair of shorts at the Gap. They were light brown and they had coral, yellow, and white tiny flowers all over them. They were very cute, and I was excited to wear them to school. In the cafeteria, I was standing and waiting for the bus after school. My bus came late, which meant I was in there by myself for a long time. The few friends I had left much earlier on their buses. So there I was by myself, and one girl came over to me with her friend in tow. My heart sank. She was repeatedly and intentionally mean to me and seemed to love embarrassing me and others. She was always kind of a mean girl in the school. She pointed to my shorts and mentioned the fact that her skinny and beautiful friend had the same pair on. She very loudly said how funny it was that we had the same shorts, except that the other girl's were probably a size two and mine were probably a size twelve or bigger. Of course I turned beat red and was totally mortified. I really felt traumatized for a long time. I got over it. But it wasn't until after college that I learned that that particular girl who had bullied me had grown up in a physically abusive household.

It really helped me understand that violence begets more violence and unkindness begets more unkindness. I know that everyone has the power to break that cycle, whether it's in families or among friends, and there are resources available to help with that. When seeking to elevate one's consciousness, it quickly becomes challenging to consciously harm another, because you can't help but imagine what it would be like to be in their shoes.

If you or a child you know is experiencing bullying, check out the recommended resources section at the end of the book.

—— *Activity* ——
Forgiving Our Bullies and Ourselves

On a spiritual level we now come to a really important activity. We have an opportunity to forgive anyone who's bullied us as well as forgive ourselves if we have ever bullied anybody or stood by and allowed someone to be bullied. Forgiveness is a powerful force. I believe it exists in a receptive state, and it is a process of surrendering. We can intend forgiveness, and that is certainly the first step in the process, but ultimately we can't force it. It is an energy all its own, with a mind and heart of its own.

Over fifteen years as a medical intuitive, I have seen many different cases and permutations of forgiveness changing people's lives. And what I have observed from all of these clients is that more often than not, it is a relaxing of the heart and a letting go of the negative or dense stuck energy in our minds or bodies that precedes the forgiveness.

In this activity, we will set the stage for forgiveness. After you've enacted this, the forgiveness itself will be able to spontaneously emerge from your soul. It will bubble forth on its own, usually in a moment of surrender.

What is this spiritual concept of surrender? Partly, it is giving up making an effort and instead giving the problem or situation over to spirit with as little attachment as possible. To spiritually surrender, you have to trust in the interconnected energy that flows through us all, whatever you call it.

To participate in this activity, you can sit or lie down somewhere quiet where you won't be disturbed for fifteen or twenty minutes. Get comfortable and close your eyes. Pay attention to your breathing and bring yourself into a calm and meditative state.

Now state aloud, "I allow any dense energy or disturbance within me to gently come to the surface for my highest good."

Tune in to what that feels like while staying in a state of nonattachment as much as you can. Notice any emotions that arise, thoughts that pop into your head, pictures you see in your mind's eye, colors you sense, impressions that you get, smells that you notice, sounds that you hear, or kinesthetic feelings that arise. Just breathe through any of these sensations or impressions.

Say aloud, "I ask Kwan Yin and Tara, the goddesses of com-passion, to help me surrender all of these burdens that I have carried to be transmuted now back into pure white light. I offer this light as fuel to power growing compassion on earth." Now breathe very deeply. Suck as much air as you can and then blow it out vigorously for as long as you can. Inhale and exhale these huge breaths quickly. Make sure they are not shallow breaths but deep breaths in which you pull all the air deep into the bottom of your lungs, feeling like you're breathing from your abdomen. Do this for a few minutes and then let it wind down when the time feels right.

Stand and say aloud, "I am in proper universal alignment, and I am filled with pure white light." Allow this universal white light to flow through you from top to bottom. It will be pump-ing pure white light through the top of your head, straight down through your body, and out your feet. This will clear out any remaining density or debris and fill any open spaces that have been cleared with white light.

Next, thank Kwan Yin and Tara. You can do this in your own words, and you can feel free to ask them to stay with you to help you with other things in your life. They are available to guide you and assist you as much as you allow them to.

Finally, say the following aloud: "I now seal and protect my energy body with pure white light, as needed, for my highest good for all time. I disconnect as needed from everyone in-volved in this meditation for my highest good."

And you are done! You have moved the energy in the body that needed to move, and now you don't need to do anything but allow the grace of forgiveness to find you. No effort is required on your part. You will experience a spontaneous moment of gentle surrender, and forgiveness will fill you. You might not even be totally aware of it when it happens, or it might be accompanied by a spiritual epiphany. It doesn't matter what the experience is because forgiveness is coming for you. And its grace and beauty are undeniable.

> *Forgiveness happens every time we surrender*
> *our attachment to pain.*
> *#thecompassionrevolution*

Day 26

Celebrities and Cyber Kindness

The Internet is the primary form of communication and information transmission in our world now. Celebrities are the new mythological figures, and celebrity gossip is the new myths. These are now the stories that are told over and over in our culture. These are the stories that go viral online. What is so compelling about these public figures? I think they represent archetypes, which are imprints of societal ideals and proclivities. Archetypes are also symbols of different parts of ourselves. There's a whole field of study called Jungian psychology that delves into it more deeply, but essentially what I mean is that celebrities are reflecting parts of ourselves. They turn up the volume on qualities that we have, and sometimes that has a polarizing effect in society.

Take the famous Kardashian family. Whatever you may think about them, they certainly are a family of powerful women. They are embodying a certain brand of feminine strength that is resonating with the cultural zeitgeist right now. Some parts of it are empowering for women, and perhaps some parts of it are putting undue emphasis on how women look and the merits of cultivating a youthful appearance. What most people can't deny is that they are part of a new mythology.

A few years ago *Cosmopolitan* put the women of the Kardashian family on the cover of its magazine. The headline said that they were the new royalty, and there was a massive and vicious Internet backlash. People were so offended! How could they compare this family to the royal family in England? The unkindness, judgment, and vitriol flew fast and furious all over the Internet for days—this is the polarizing nature of extreme celebrity in our culture.

People are fascinated by celebrities, but they are also a little too thrilled when celebrities fail or have problems. And that's what I want to talk about. I want to open the discussion about why humans feel they get a boost in superiority from the suffering of someone else, in this case a celebrity. I think this speaks to the shadow part of all of us and our culture. It's the part of us that is insecure, needy, and ashamed and doesn't feel we're good enough. That is the part within many of us that watches with fascination as a rock star behaves badly or when a famous actor is diagnosed with a fatal disease.

The thing about the shadow self is that it only has power when you don't look at it. As we learned in a previous chapter, when you face your shadow, become aware of it, embrace it, and integrate it, you experience greater wholeness. That is cultivating compassion through different levels of self-awareness and stepping into consciousness. And every single person has the power to choose consciousness in each moment. And if we make a misstep, NBD (no big deal). The moment will end, and we can choose again. It's that simple.

So the next time you see a celebrity gossip story or somebody tells you about one, take a moment to imagine what it's like to be that person. And, yes, I'm sure there are good parts, but imagine walking down the street and getting mobbed by hundreds of loud photographers while you are carrying your new baby, who is crying because the noise is frightening him. Just let yourself develop empathy for celebrities. Understand that although these stories may be the new mythology, they are being lived by regular human beings. And in creating a compassionate world, everyone is included, no matter how envious you might be of their figure or their money. Know that it's likely that there's someone else somewhere who at some point in your life will look up to you and think that you are the ideal. There's someone who might be coveting your life and thinking it is amazing. Wouldn't you like them to think, speak, and act compassionately toward you? Wouldn't you like them to treat you with respect and kindness and not be fascinated by your suffering?

That Username Is a Real Person

In a world where our identities online can feel real, it's important to remember that a username is a real person. We post so much of our lives online now. We share pictures. We share our favorite inspirational quotes. We share status updates and reviews of books and movies we like. Some people post pictures of their most fashionable outfits or their favorite makeup routines. Some people share passages from their favorite books or poems. And because of this, we are online all the time. There is more of a Wild West mentality online. People say whatever they want. They don't necessarily worry about someone's feelings. The old saying "If you don't have something nice to say, don't say anything at all" is a great one to live by in your online life. You might not love that picture of someone's breakfast, but they may have taken half an hour to get the perfect shot, find just the right filter, and come up with the cleverest caption they could. Your comments (positive or negative) might mean the world to them.

Our online way of life can be isolating. Although we can't change that for everyone, we can certainly make a conscious effort to spread the love and positivity through our online pursuits.

Online Inferiority Complexes and Other Signs of a Troll

Do you wonder about Internet trolls? Do you ever wonder why they spend time talking so negatively online? Who would take the time to go on someone's blog and post something disrespectful? Or something derogatory? What do they get out of it?

It's very similar to the questions we asked earlier about bullying. And I think the answer is similar. They are seeking a boost-up feeling that tells them they're better than someone else. But it's a fallacy. It's not real. Anything that gains something by diminishing something else is a false gain. It's empty. It's lifeless. It has no energy imbued within it except that which is dense and heavy.

So in the land of empathy and compassion we might surmise that the people who take the time to be Internet trolls have pretty sad lives. And even if their lives seem great on the outside, they must be hurting on the inside. They must need to feel a sense of power and accomplishment. They must be living from a stance of competition as opposed to compassion. That's really too bad. Because when someone is negative like that, it makes less space for authentic positive experiences in their lives. They're letting part of their shadow consume them and drive them and their actions. They're seeking that feeling of control that we talked about in the bullying section, except clearly they are being controlled by their own inner demons. That's really what the shadow self is—inner demons.

I always figure that Internet trolls have massive inferiority complexes. How challenging that must be, to feel so small and insignificant on the inside and to value oneself so little that cutting down others anonymously and in a cowardly way online provides some fleeting dose of relief.

If you ever deal with an Internet troll on your blog or your social media, just try to remember that pain begets more pain until someone breaks the cycle. And maybe you are the person with the courage to do it. Maybe you're the person with the courage to ignore the troll. And even forgive them. Author Gabby Bernstein often says, "Forgive and delete." That is her philosophy on dealing with trolls on her site. We can all take a page from that.

Public Is the New Private

Can you believe that the Internet is so popular after only about twenty-five years of mainstream use? Never in the known history of humanity has something so quickly and pervasively changed our culture. And with this massive change has come a flood of new conditions and situations for us all to manage as best we can.

One example of this is that twenty years ago when you applied for a job, you didn't have to worry about your employer searching for you online and finding embarrassing pictures or disparaging commentary. Now a successful life requires a full-time media curation effort—public is the new private.

For example, ten years ago, I had someone stalk me briefly. Luckily, they were unable to find my home address. Now it's public information with just a few clicks, and the world is very different. These changes in the way our culture and society function require flexibility and creative problem-solving. In some cases they may also require courage. We have to look life in the face and not be afraid. We have to trust that we are safe and that we can capably care for ourselves and keep ourselves safe.

Back in 2003, I was writing a book and consulting with my spirit guides. I work a lot with certain archangels personally and in my medical intuitive practice. At the time my archangel guides told me that the advent of the Internet meant the end of secrets. I had the sense at the time that that would be largely positive, but we're certainly seeing how it does take some getting used to. And the longer we've been alive, the more we remember that pre-Internet time before 1995. That means we have more acclimating to do in the world where public is the new private. There are no more secrets. Or very few. Will this ultimately lead to greater transparency? If we apply the tenets of compassion, empathy, and caring to everything we do, we can navigate whatever life brings.

—— *Activity* ——
Spread the Love Online

Every day we have an opportunity to spread love online. Today let's do it together! I'm going to issue you a challenge. I want you to use an app of your choosing (Twitter, Facebook, Instagram, Snapchat, or Pinterest) to create a picture collage of compassion. It can be moments of compassion from your daily life, pictures that remind you of compassion, or works of art that you feel inspire compassion. Just create a collage of images of beauty around the theme of compassion. And you can even put the word "compassion" on your piece of virtual art. Hashtag it #thecompassionrevolution, and we can all search that hashtag and share these beautiful collages to spread the idea of compassion online. Make sure you use that hashtag and search for my compassion collages! I have made you a bunch!

Remember, that username is a real person.
Choose to spread the love online.
#thecompassionrevolution

Day 27

Live to Give

Have you noticed that there are two types of attitudes about money in life? There are people who seem to worry about it a lot and people who do not. And what I've noticed is that those two types of people don't necessarily have the obvious amount of income to go with their worry level.

On the one hand, I can think of several schoolteachers that I know who live on very little and behave and have the attitude that they are extremely abundant. You never hear them griping about money. You can tell they're not worried about it. And they still manage to do everything that they want. To take that to the next level, some of them give their time and a little bit of their money to charity on a very regular basis.

On the other hand, I know plenty of upper-middle-class people who do worry about money all the time. They're concerned about having enough of it. And I'll admit I worry about it sometimes. I think everybody does. But the really interesting and distinct difference between these two types of people is the attitude that they project. The first type feels abundant on the inside because these people have a rich life and a healthy emotional foundation. The second type feels lack on the inside, and so they're in fear of lack in their external world. Those people are lacking a sense of emotional safety on the inside, and really they are lacking a feeling of abundance of spirit. There are endless combinations of different degrees of these two types in all of us. We may feel abundant sometimes and like we are lacking sometimes.

The truth is that we all have the opportunity to feel abundant. In the Western world, we all have the opportunity to reframe the way we look at our lives and see how amazingly rich we are. Tackle the problem of feeling like you're living in lack instead of abundance, and dive deeply into your own emotional issues. Unravel the energy of lack from your mental, emotional, and physical energy bodies.

That may take many different forms, including the following:

+ Feeling like you didn't get enough attention.

+ Feeling like you didn't have enough money available as a child to have the same clothes as other people or to be able to do the same things, like buy candy after school.

+ If your family lived in poverty, and so you didn't always have enough food or the electricity would go out.

+ If you got the message that you weren't worth much due to the words and actions of the people in your life.

+ If you got the message that you weren't important.

In a case like not feeling important as a child, that might mean that you had plenty of money but your parents were always going on vacation without you and leaving you with babysitters. The inner child takes those actions as a message that the person is not that important.

When we talk about all of these situations and feelings, what we are really talking about feeling is the lack of love. All of those situations translate into feeling unloved and to feeling needy for more love.

Imagine this scenario: A little girl grows up in a lower-middle-class family in Indiana. She has a roof over her head and always has food and shelter. Her parents are not the warmest people. They're not into overt displays of affection. They do not say "I love you" to her or hug her. As she gets older, her father moves up in his job as a construction worker and begins to make a more decent wage. He squirrels it away, never sharing it with the family, and then eventually he uses it to buy a boat that he can take his friends fishing on in the local lake. Meanwhile, this little girl has grown into a teenager, but she doesn't get any help with her college savings, her car, the money needed for field trips or class trips, or her prom dress. She has to work to get all of these things herself. If her parents were trying to teach her a strong work ethic but were very loving and affectionate toward her, she would never have gotten the message that she wasn't worth very much. But she did. By being emotionally unavailable and financially withholding, her parents' actions and attitudes gave the girl a message early in her life that she was unworthy.

As a result of feeling so unworthy as a child, as an adult she never felt that she had the power to change her life. She never felt that she was worthy of taking action to affect what she wanted. The message that she got was that she wasn't worthy of much effort. In this imaginary scenario are those parents horrible evil villains? No. They're just people making their way in the world. Maybe they were not planning to have children. Maybe they realized after the fact that it wasn't what they wanted. Maybe their parents treated them that way, so that's just all they knew. Emotional wounds that we take on from our families of origin are rarely delivered intentionally. More often than not they are just wrought by people living an unconscious life.

But here is the key point in all of that: at any moment in any place, we all have the power to take ownership of our lives and change them. At any point the young woman in this imaginary scenario could do one of a number of things to try to unravel what was holding her back from the greatness that she could be living.

That is our real issue with feeling lack of love and the energy of lack—it holds us back from achieving our greatness. It holds us back from living our calling. Some people call that our life's mission, or our *dharma* in Buddhist philosophy. It is in living our calling that we find true fulfillment and true emotional abundance, and it often leads to material abundance as well.

When we live our calling, we are giving and receiving in perfect balance. We are in service to life. And everyone's calling is different. The hairdresser who makes hundreds of people per year feel beautiful while talking to them and delivering positive messages that illuminate things in their mind is living her calling. She's changing lives in this case, one person at a time. The financial advisor who helps people plan for their retirement so they can be safe and secure throughout their old age is living her calling. She is helping people create a better quality of life every day.

The common denominator in living one's calling is loving what you do most of the time. I'll share a personal example. I honestly love generating ideas for books. I get so jazzed up about my next idea. I love writing the book proposal! The possibilities are endless, spanning out before me to the horizon and beyond. I do also love the process of writing books. I love that I'm getting to share this information with you right now. I have to admit that sometimes when I'm on a book deadline, have to get things done fast, and have a lot of other things going on, it's not always fun 100 percent of the time. But it's fun most of the time. And beyond that I know that I am living my calling at this moment. When we have that awareness in fleeting moments throughout our life, we are in the flow. We are giving the best and most wonderful thing we can give to life—our true service—and it doesn't mean we don't get paid for it. That's the beauty of this.

When we line up with our life's mission, we can live to give. But we will be rich in so many ways. When we're in the flow and giving what we're meant to be giving to society, we will be in the energy of abundance. We can't help but be in this energy of abundance because we're living our dharma. And abundance is what it really means to be rich; it is not only money. Abundance is also an abundance of love and happiness and connection. Abundance is also lots of fun with friends. It's the richness of life. It's delicious food. It's spontaneous laughter. It's hugs and cuddling. It's beautiful music and art giving you pleasure. It's all of these things and more.

Think back to the example earlier of the philanthropic teacher with the abundant attitude. This teacher is living her dharma! She is living her life's mission. Every day she's touching the lives of children with the most positive attitude, and she feels abundant. She might not have piles of money. But she has everything she needs and the attitude of abundance fills her. She lives to give, and she is rich.

Don't think for any minute that you have to live on a small teacher's salary to be living your calling. Your calling might be to be a multimillion-dollar company's CEO. Your calling might be separate from your career. You might have a career that you enjoy but your real calling is the volunteer work you do on the weekend. The permutations and possibilities are endless. So don't get hung up on the details. Just know that you must step into your greatness to be truly rich.

So use the phrase "live to give" as a contemplation prompt. How can you give today? How can you be in service to goodness today? When we give, it inspires a feeling of gratitude in us for what we have, and gratitude attracts more of the good things in life.

—— *Activity* ——
Live to Give

I'm going to challenge you to do something in the realm of giving. Anything you want. You can go in your community and do something that you know is needed, like trash cleanup or collecting for a food bank, or you can take the time to write a handwritten, loving card to a family member who you know could use a pick-me-up. Your giving can be local or global. But today, give to someone. Every time you give, you line up more closely with your dharma, or your calling.

—— *Activity* ——
Daily Gratitude

Tonight before bed, pull out your journal. In your journal make a list of thirty things you are grateful for. It can be absolutely anything, from your family to the sunlight on your skin as you got in your car this morning to the roller-skating date you have scheduled with friends this weekend. Watch how your outlook subtly but powerfully changes! Notice how this feeling of gratitude permeates your life when you start to focus on it. Tell me what you are grateful for and what you notice! And use the hashtag #thecompassionrevolution.

Live to give and be rich of heart and laughter.
#thecompassionrevolution

Day 28

Stop Being Snarky and Start Living

Everyone feels unsure of themselves sometimes. Everyone feels vulnerable or insecure sometimes. We live in a world that can sometimes be hostile and hurtful, and so the urge to defend ourselves is real. We feel this urge to varying degrees. Some people feel it all the time because they never felt safe as a child, let alone as an adult. Some people don't feel it very often and just wear their heart on their sleeve, wide open and available to the world.

Every human deserves the experience of feeling emotionally safe. Emotional safety happens when you feel safe on the inside. You feel that you are okay. You even love yourself. And you also trust yourself. You trust that you can provide the care and compassion needed to have a good life.

Feeling safe on the inside also means that your foundation is solid. Ideally, we would all have an emotionally nourishing and unconditionally loving childhood, though it does not always happen that way for everyone. In fact, it doesn't happen for many people, realistically. But if your deep, internal foundation is solid, it means that you have done the work needed to rehabilitate your inner child. You've gotten yourself to the point where you do feel emotionally safe. And from there you can soar.

Sadly, this feeling of emotional safety is not present in that many of us all the time, and one of the places this lack is presented is online. Have you ever seen comments written by people who you can tell just take pride in being snarky? It often seems like they are clearly trying to be clever, but not authentically clever—overly and superiorly clever. This attitude is coming from what I would call a really mentally based place instead of a heart-centered place. And we have all done it! I know I have. It's a basic part of human nature to desire to feel superior to someone else. Especially if we don't feel good enough. If we are having a tough time in our job we might unconsciously interact with others in a vaguely snarky way. We are not being overtly malevolent. We don't have a conscious desire to be negative. But still, the negativity is there.

And now we live in a society that seems to prize snarkiness. Articles making snarky comments about women's physiques or celebrities' misdeeds are the norm instead of the exception. Unfortunately, we are taking the easy road, the road where we can dissociate from our hearts and our souls and instead focus on that which is negative and escapist.

No matter how many celebrity news blogs we read, we find that we feel empty when we behave this way. When we read about things that are just snarky, there's an emptiness after. Our soul is not responding. Our level of consciousness is not raising and is maybe even lowering. When we are truly conscious and in a heart-centered place, compassion is our true nature. And snarkily laughing while we read about a pop star's latest legal trouble isn't compassionate. It's not loving or benevolent to take pleasure and entertainment from somebody else being down.

And that is the crux of the snarky epidemic in our culture. It is the snide comments that a friend makes about another friend. It's that age-old pastime of gossip. It is all of these things that are seductive because they give us a quick boost that we might be better than the person that we're talking about. But of course we're not. And we're taking the quick and easy path instead of the more thoughtful, compassionate, consciousness-driven path.

The good news is we have the opportunity to make a different choice at any time. So notice those moments when you might've chosen the snarky side of life. You might've engaged someone in a conversation about a snarky news article you just read. Instead, you could make a different choice. Instead, you could choose to talk about the wonderful deeds of a mutual friend or organizing a trash cleanup in your neighborhood instead of gossiping. You have an endless array of possibilities before you that are positive choices. They really don't require that much effort to find. And they really require only a modicum of effort to select as consistent and desirable behaviors in your life.

Some people might wonder about this choice. What's in it for me? What do I get out of being less snarky and more compassionate?

What you get out of it is soul food. You get honest-to-goodness food for your soul. The soul is this amazing, indefinable part of us. We use the word in many different ways in our culture. But what I mean by "soul" in this case is the part of you that's deep within and yet permeates your whole being and your whole life. It is connected to the energy of the universe, and people might call that your spirit as well. The thing that I think is unique about the soul is that it's the spirit woven and intertwined with the human heart and human emotion. It gives the spirit a heart. It gives the neutral aspect of spirit a personalized, personified heart energy. Soul equals spirit plus caring.

The soul in these terms is the birthplace of compassion. If you meditate long enough and put your attention on compassion long enough, this caring and soul-level awareness bubbles up out of you. And it's not just separate from your humanity. It's not some spiritual part of you up in the sky. It's here incarnate on earth in your body and imbued with emotion and spiritual energy. I believe that our calling as a race is to attain this soul concept. It is where we are going as we raise our consciousness and vibration as humans.

It is very much worth cultivating our soul! Because when we do, our lives become richer. They become abundant, pleasurable, meaningful experiences. And I believe that that is why we choose to come here and incarnate on earth at all, to have these meaningful soul experiences. These are rich, diverse, poignant experiences filled with everything from service and helping others to deep belly laughter to hugging and caring for one another to enjoying the beauty of our planet to quiet moments in contemplation. In my opinion, truly raising our consciousness while incarnated in a human body can lead to deep experiences of our soul.

The soul is not snarky. It doesn't have any need to defend or enhance itself or to make itself feel superior. It already knows it is divinity. It already has a full, loving heart. It transcends all the snark and instead finds the depth and meaning in life.

—— *Activity* ——
Rejecting Snarkiness and Redirecting Our Energy to the Soul

In this activity we're going to take some concrete steps to help us joyfully let go of any snarkiness and gossip and instead embrace the privilege of cultivating our soul's energy. You will need a journal and a quiet place to sit down and contemplate for about fifteen or twenty minutes.

Get comfortable with your journal and take a few minutes to breathe in and center yourself. Try to calm and quiet your mind. Use deep breathing for this. If you need to repeat a mantra for two or three minutes to slow things down, choose the word "soul" today. Repeat the word "soul" over and over anytime your mind wanders from noticing your breathing. When you watch your breathing, what you really do is just bring your attention to the whoosh of air as it comes in your mouth or nose and moves down into your lungs and back up and out. It is something to focus on instead of your thoughts. And the breath in our body is often thought in some yogic traditions to also be our *prana*, or our life-force energy. Deepening your breathing brings more oxygen and life force into your body, which is good for your health.

Once you have calmed and quieted your mind, get your journal. Take a moment to reflect on the following question and write the first thing that comes to your mind: Do you need to be lifted up so you feel better about yourself?

Look at what you wrote. A lot of us might answer yes to that question, because we don't feel perfect all the time. It's okay that we feel that way. We can keep doing the work of loving ourselves like we would love a treasured friend or family member. We can continue treating ourselves with the utmost care and self-respect to cultivate greater feelings of worthiness.

Next, ask yourself another question and write down the first thing that comes to mind: In the last five years have I succumbed to the urge to in some way diminish another to make myself feel a little better?

There's no judgment here. Reread your answer and accept what you may have done. I have done it. In an incident several years ago I did that with just one unconscious sentence. And to be honest I perseverate over it to this day because I feel so bad about it. For me, part of the work is letting go of that, forgiving myself, and trying to think about what I could do to put more positive energy back into the situation than I took out of it at the time with negativity. Perhaps this is the work of consciousness, watching ourselves and being aware of ourselves and then making course corrections when we veer off track from compassion.

Now, in your journal ask yourself if you have ever used snarkiness to feel more accepted in a social situation. Answer honestly whatever comes to mind.

Freewrite about all of this. How do you feel about these choices? Remember, it's not about judging yourself or punishing yourself—certainly not. It's just about bringing awareness to yourself, accepting yourself, and learning from situations that arise in your life. I always ask myself, where can I do better? That doesn't mean that I did poorly. It doesn't mean that I'm not good enough. It means I strive for excellence. That's why I wanted to write a book about compassion—because I want to cultivate it in my life.

Continue your freewriting for a while and just kind of explore your thoughts and feelings about everything. Take a few minutes and contemplate these two sentences: Compassion is given freely with no expectation of reward. Compassion is choosing to be conscious and cultivate empathy and positivity in every possible moment.

After reading the sentences and using them as contemplation prompts, I want you to write down one or more affirmative statements about what you want to do differently after becoming more aware of this topic in your life. Some examples are "I choose to be caring and compassionate and think about other people's feelings before I speak" or "I choose to only speak positively about other people."

After you create your one or more affirmative statements, think about how you can commit to enacting them. Do you need a reminder somewhere, like a Post-it note on your bathroom mirror? Do you need a little slip of paper in your wallet to see it periodically throughout the day? Do you need to make it a wallpaper on the lock screen of your phone? How can you make this a sustained change in your behavior? Remind yourself what you get out of it. You'll get a deeper, richer experience of life and warm feelings in your heart. You'll get emotional abundance and emotional safety out of choosing compassion and consciousness as much as possible.

Compassion is given freely with no expectation of reward.
#thecompassionrevolution

Day 29

Ideas Plus People Equal a Movement

The time is now for a movement centered on compassion. It's not tomorrow or next month. We need it now. Our world needs it now. And we can all be a part of the change. Change is inevitable. It can't be stopped. But we can guide the direction of it every day through our thoughts and actions.

Personal responsibility need not be a drag but a privilege. What we do matters! Every look, every word of caring, and every kind gesture make a difference and build a world based on love. Love is the opposite of fear and illuminates the hearts of all it touches. This is how fear falls away. It just gets dimmer. And when the big changes come and fear flares again, we are ready. We are centered in loving compassion for ourselves and others. A compassionate world is waiting. Let's step into it.

Why do we need a compassion movement now?

+ Of all adults, 66 percent suffer from "nomophobia," the fear of being without a mobile device.

- There has been a 1,200 percent increase in the reporting of anxiety disorders since 1980.
- According to one study, 48 percent of people have reported lying awake at night due to stress.
- In the United States $300 billion is lost in annual costs to employers in stress-related health care and missed work.

Our world is sorely in need and compassion is the way to help each other and ourselves. Why?

- Compassion relieves stress.
- Kindness fosters connection and alleviates feelings of loneliness and isolation.
- Caring for others gives life meaning.
- Nurturing yourself raises levels of personal comfort.
- Experiences of interconnection inspire feelings of joy and happiness.

As I wrote this book I asked myself, how does one person create a global movement? It was a daunting question. Certainly a lofty aspiration. You want to talk about idealism? This idea was the height of idealism. But I do want to create a movement. I want to inspire as many people as possible to choose the positive in life. That's why I wrote a book about joy, and that's why I wrote this book about compassion. As I told you in the introduction of this book, I want an end to suffering. That's my end goal for all life. And to be honest I don't even know if that's a possibility in millions of years. Part of my spiritual journey is meditating, questioning, and talking to spirit helpers to try to understand if that's possible here on earth. Here on earth we are living in duality. We are spiritual beings, or souls incarnated in physical bodies, living in a physical world. And in this world, animals eat other animals and plants. Some things have to die so others can live. Do they suffer? They might. In my experience as an intuitive, animals have rich emotional lives. And so do plants, although they have a different flavor than we as humans might be used to.

I don't pretend to have all the answers. And I don't believe in gurus. I think we've entered the age of everyone becoming their own guru. But we do have spiritual teachers, just like we have teachers at school who teach us how to read and write and do trigonometry. We have teachers who can help us learn to meditate and talk to guides or feel the interconnected life force all around us. In my life, I'm seeking to understand how to make not just the world but the universe and multiverse, which is an idea of many infinite, never-ending universes in the cosmos, better. That's my quest. I suppose as a soul I could not have picked a better classroom than this planet! I suspect that many of you who are reading this book are on a similar quest, whether you define it in cosmic terms, like I do, or more practical terms, like you are searching for meaning in your existence and you'd like to create a better world for your children.

Although we don't have the answers and might not have them while we are here in a physical body, we have the opportunity to try to effect change. And we can do this with a certain level of nonattachment. We can do it with an eye toward empathic caring, and we can exercise our compassion while striving to accept what is and change what we can for the better.

So let's create a movement together! On my website Amy LeighMercree.com just click on the page titled "The Compassion Revolution" and join the movement. We have a Facebook group, we have Twitter campaigns, and we also have links that show ways you can help. I'm asking you to post on our Facebook page and share ideas and links so that people can help in your community. Tell us ways that we can exercise our compassion for your community. I'm here in the eastern half of the United States trying to make a difference in my community, and there are probably many of you miles away who are doing the same thing all over the world. Many of the people who pick up this book would like to help the other members of this community. These acts of compassion do not have to involve money. They can be large acts, like one by a restaurant owner in India who puts a fridge outside her restaurant and stocks it every day with free meals for the homeless. The rest of her neighborhood joined in, and now the free meal fridge is stocked with over two hundred free meals a day. Or your act of compassion can be small, like posting on our Facebook page about a local swim team that doesn't have funding for new uniforms. Who knows if an up-and-coming sport swimsuit designer might like to donate?

Far beyond the Facebook page and the community created by this book, you can answer the call within you to express your greatness in the world and spread compassion. Don't forget, modeling compassion and empathetic behavior that is positive for the people in your life and in your community is powerful. Just choosing to speak, think, and act from a place of compassion creates powerful ripples in the world around you. Understand that you matter. Each thing you do matters so much. Embrace that personal responsibility and start using your creativity and your idealism for good.

—— *Activity* ——
How Can You Create a Compassion Movement in Your Community?

In this activity you will journal in response to some contemplation prompts. So grab your journal and find a quiet space, and let's get started. Answer the following questions in your journal.

For these first questions think about the next thirty days.

+ How much time per week would you like to devote to spreading compassion?

- Would you enjoy this more if it were a solitary or social pursuit?

- Do you feel called this month to make a local, global, or somewhere-in-between compassion effort?

- What are the top three issues in our world that you feel most called to help with? Some examples are climate change, closing the wage gap, improving the educational system, supporting the arts for children and adults, and ending world hunger.

- Would you rather volunteer with an established organization or create your own guerrilla compassion initiatives?

- Do you feel more called to share your caring with people in your life or with strangers?

Answer these questions on a long-term scale.

- Do you ever aspire to hold a greater leadership position in your community, or are you more interested in a behind the scenes role?

- Do you hope to be able to leave behind a legacy of compassion or philanthropy after you transition from this world?

- Are you interested in short-term or lifelong service to humanity or both?

Answer the following questions with the first thing that comes to your mind in a loose way.

- ✦ What is holding you back from devoting some of your time toward charity?
- ✦ What stops you from speaking up for compassionate causes or in situations where more compassion is needed?
- ✦ What might happen if you put your focus on compassion for ten minutes a day?
- ✦ How can you overcome any obstacles that are stopping you from living a more compassionate life?
- ✦ What talents do you have that you love sharing? Some examples are making collages, painting, singing with children, crunching numbers, talking on the phone, and being a people person.

Answering these questions will help you get prepared to be a part of a grassroots, probably under-the-radar compassion movement building in our world right now. These are designed as a jumping-off point to help you contemplate what you might enjoy doing or saying to help others.

The real intention of this chapter is to inspire you to begin taking action in your life to further the cause of the light. The light contains goodness, compassion, caring, empathy, joy, love, and more. You can spread the love and positivity every day. And you can be a part of a growing movement to share compassion with the world.

Start a compassion movement in your community
by being a living example of kindness.
#thecompassionrevolution

Day 30

Join In—
Everyone Is Welcome

Back in 2003 I lived in Maui in a resort community. There were a lot of tourists and people who would come to Hawaii in the winter for a month or more at a time. There was a group of retirees who were always out on the shuffleboard court, and for the entire month of March this one really cute older man would go out onto the court at about eight o'clock every morning and yell, "Shuffleboard! Anyone is welcome!"

He would gather his playmates! And it always worked. People heard him and knew it was time to go have their community game. It was quite a lively social scene because of him, and I really like the inclusive model he created. "Anyone is welcome." What a great credo. We need that philosophy to permeate our culture right now.

In the endeavor of creating a welcoming world we can start by seeding that energy of welcome within ourselves. If it feels right to you, repeat this affirmation to bolster the energy of welcome in your life now: "I am welcomed with open arms everywhere I go. All of existence embraces me with the knowledge that we are all one. Love is my guide. Love stewards my life, so each moment of my existence is one of pure welcome for all time."

Participation in life is what creates miracles. It is what creates enjoyment. And ultimately, it's also what creates change when change is needed. Compassion can absolutely be a static state. It is valuable to sit in meditation and focus on compassion. And even the act of radiating the energy of compassion is actually an action. That in itself is extremely valuable!

But even more than passive action, in this talk of creating a compassion movement, direct action for the cause of compassion can be catalyzing and transformative for each of us personally and for parts of our world. When we choose to make the effort and put our attention on something completely, energy follows attention, and action springs forth from attention. There is a business adage shared by my father-in-law that "what gets attention gets done." And it is certainly true. So when you put your attention on compassion and then even further on the idea of taking small, regular actions to promote the cause of compassion in our world, amazing things can happen. Let's commit to this cause today. As a community of human universal citizens, we have the opportunity to leave not only our planet but our universe better than how we found it when we incarnated in the bodies we are in right now. We matter, each and every one of us. And each and every one of us has the power to effect change.

—— *Activity* ——
The Pledge of Compassion

Take the pledge of compassion with me today. To do this simply read the words below and really let them permeate your being. Really use them as a chance to contemplate the power that you wield as a citizen of the earth. Begin by reading this pledge to yourself. And then if it resonates with you, say it aloud with vigor and harness the power of your own intention to make the living energy of compassion a reality in your life. And if part of it resonates with you and part of it does not, then just say the parts that you like.

See what resonates for you. Then speak aloud your pledge and join me in working toward an end to suffering through the energy of compassion and positivity.

The Pledge of Compassion

Compassion permeates my being.

Compassion follows me.

Compassion precedes me.

Compassion is within me.

I apply my conscious attention to the task of spreading compassion and positivity in each moment for my highest good.

I offer the perfect amount of attention and energy, for my highest good, in joyful service of the light of compassion.

I am compassion.

May the earth be wrapped in the energy of compassion and love for all time.

It is done.

The beauty of compassion is free, and everyone is welcome to it.
#thecompassionrevolution

Conclusion

Thank you so much for taking this journey with me into the heart of compassion! I am honored that you are here. I am going to sum up a few key points that I learned in my thirty-day quest to understand compassion.

Among the many takeaway lessons we can discover from this thirty-day endeavor, one important thing I learned is that daily commitment is truly profound. If you put your attention on something every day for a month, it's pretty close to becoming a habit. By making compassion a habit, you build up the muscle of empathy and caring. As we discussed way back in the introduction to this book, if you're already a caretaker, that may not be a muscle that necessarily needs tons of building in you. In your case, that would mean the muscle that does need building is the one for self-compassion. You have to have the basic strength of really strong self-compassion to be able to extend true, healthy, and effective compassion to the world.

The great thing is that by taking a thirty-day practice, as demonstrated in this book, we can be guided in making a daily commitment to compassion. Now that you have finished the book, you can make yet another thirty-day commitment to compassion! Make this a movement in your life, and the energy that you create by doing so will spill over into the lives of those around you.

I wrote this book to be a part of an eventual end to suffering and as a love letter to our planet and our universe. It's my way of saying I care deeply, and every single person, plant, animal, stone, molecule, and atom matters to me. All life matters, and I meditate, pray, and wish for happiness, health, and joy for us all.

I hope your life was enhanced by our thirty days together, and I hope you stay in touch with me through social media and my website and events. Let's work together to create a more compassionate planet.

Compassion Toolkit

Want more information on compassion? To download your free compassion toolkit and put what you've learned in this book into action right now, go to www.AmyLeighMercree.com /compassiontoolkit (password: COMPASSION).

Recommended Resources

Amy Leigh Mercree, *A Little Bit of Meditation: An Introduction to Mindfulness*

Amy Leigh Mercree, *Joyful Living: 101 Ways to Transform Your Spirit and Revitalize Your Life*

Amy Leigh Mercree and Chad Mercree, *A Little Bit of Chakras: An Introduction to Energy Healing*

Chad Mercree, *A Little Bit of Buddha: An Introduction to Buddhist Thought*

Dalai Lama, *Beyond Religion: Ethics for a Whole World*

Dalai Lama, *The Art of Happiness: A Handbook for Living*

Doreen Virtue, *The Lightworker's Way: Awakening Your Spiritual Power to Know and Heal*

Edward M. Hallowell and John J. Ratey, *Driven to Distraction*

Elaine N. Aron, *The Highly Sensitive Person: How to Thrive When the World Overwhelms You*

Emma Mildon, *The Soul Searcher's Handbook: A Modern Girl's Guide to the New Age World*

Mark Epstein, *Going to Pieces without Falling Apart: A Buddhist Perspective on Wholeness*

Shannon Kaiser, *Adventures for Your Soul: 21 Ways to Transform Your Habits and Reach Your True Potential* and *Find Your Happy: An Inspirational Guide to Loving Life to Its Fullest*

For Bullying

DoSomething.org, https://www.dosomething.org/us

PACER Center's Kids Against Bullying, http://www .pacerkidsagainstbullying.org/kab/

StopBullying.gov, https://stopbullying.gov

Mark C. Purcell and Jason R. Murphy, *Mindfulness for Teen Anger: A Workbook to Overcome Anger and Aggression Using MBSR and DBT Skills*

Raychelle Cassada Lohmann and Julia V. Taylor, *The Bullying Workbook for Teens: Activities to Help You Deal with Social Aggression and Cyberbullying*

Bibliography

Day 1

Peschke, Ingrid. "Real Answers about Anxiety." *Changing Tides of Health* (blog), August 22, 2012. http://www.mass healthblog.com/2012/08/27/answers-to-anxiety-on-the -rise/.

Usigan, Ysolt. "5 Reasons to Make Time for Cuddling." *Shape*. Accessed January 3, 2017. http://www.shape.com/lifestyle /sex-and-love/5-health-reasons-make-time-cuddling.

Day 2

Begley, Sharon. "In the Age of Anxiety, Are We All Mentally Ill?" Reuters. July 13, 2012. http://www.reuters.com/article /us-usa-health-anxiety-idUSBRE86C07820120713.

Day 11

Ahuja, Masuma. "Teens Are Spending More Time Consuming Media, on Mobile Devices." *Washington Post*, March 13, 2013. http://www.washingtonpost.com/postlive/teens-are

-spending-more-time-consuming-media-on-mobile-devices /2013/03/12/309bb242-8689-11e2-98a3-b3db6b9ac586 _story.html.

eMarketer. "Digital Set to Surpass TV in Time Spent with US Media." eMarketer, August 1, 2013. http://www .emarketer.com/Article/Digital-Set-Surpass-TV-Time -Spent-with-US-Media/1010096.

Kleinman, Alexis. "Americans Will Spend More Time on Digital Devices Than Watching TV This Year: Research." *Huffington Post*, August 1, 2013. http://www.huffingtonpost .com/2013/08/01/tv-digital-devices_n_3691196.html.

PicMonkey. "PicMonkey Survey Finds Nearly Half of U.S. Adults Have Taken a 'Selfie;' Miley Cyrus Posts Most Entertaining 'Selfie' Images." PicMonkey press release, February 6, 2013. MarketWired. http://www.marketwired.com/press -release/picmonkey-survey-finds-nearly-half-us-adults -have-taken-selfie-miley-cyrus-posts-most-1876623.htm.

"Selfie." Merriam-Webster.com. Accessed January 3, 2017. https://www.merriam-webster.com/dictionary/selfie.

Sturt, David, and Todd Nordstrom. "The 'Selfie': Mental Disorder or Insight to Getting Better Results?" *Forbes*, April 29, 2014. http://www.forbes.com/sites/davidsturt /2014/04/29/the-selfie-mental-disorder-or-insight-to -getting-better-results/.

Thomas, Liz, and Paul Revoir. "Computers and TV Take Up Half Our Lives as We Spend Seven Hours a Day Using Technology." DailyMail.com. Last modified August 19, 2010. http://www.dailymail.co.uk/news/article-1304266/We-spend-7-hours-day-using-technology-computers-TV-lives.html.

Day 16

DoYogaWithMe. "Yoga Styles." Accessed July 20, 2016. https://www.doyogawithme.com/types-of-yoga.

Fuller, Sue. "Yoga Practice—Compassionate Poses." *Kindred Spirit Magazine*. Last modified June 30, 2015. http://kindredspirit.co.uk/yoga-practice-compassionate-poses/.

Give Back Yoga Foundation. "Biff Mithoefer: How Yin Yoga Can Help Veterans Practice Self-Compassion." Last modified August 18, 2013. http://givebackyoga.org/biff-mithoefer-how-yin-yoga-can-help-veterans-practice-self-compassion/.

Millen, Emily. "Lessons From the Yoga Sutra: 3 Ways to Call Upon Compassion." Gaia. Last modified February 3, 2014. http://www.gaia.com/article/lessons-yoga-sutras-3-ways-call-upon-compassion.

Rosen, Richard. "Who Was Patanjali?" Yoga Journal. Last modified August 28, 2014. http://www.yogajournal.com/article/philosophy/who-was-patanjali/.

Day 20

Asociación RUVID. "Dopamine Regulates the Motivation to Act, Study Shows." ScienceDaily. January 10, 2013. http://www.sciencedaily.com/releases/2013/01/130110094415.htm.

Brookshire, Bethany. "Dopamine Is _____." *Slate*, July 3, 2013. http://www.slate.com/articles/health_and_science/science/2013/07/what_is_dopamine_love_lust_sex_addiction_gambling_motivation_reward.html.

Rainoshek, David. "How Facebook (FB) is Altering Your Mind." DavidRainoshek.com. June 12, 2013. http://davidrainoshek.com/2013/06/how-facebook-fb-is-altering-your-mind-2/.

ScienceDaily. "Dopamine." Accessed April 18, 2016. http://www.sciencedaily.com/articles/d/dopamine.htm.

Day 21

Amin, Ibrahim. "Perspectives on Islam." Oxford Centre for Islamic Studies. Dalai Lama Centre for Compassion. August 17, 2015. http://compassionoxford.com/perspectives-on-compassion-in-islam/.

Beckett, John. "A Pagan View of Compassion." Under the Ancient Oaks: Musings of a Pagan, Druid and Unitarian Universalist, *Patheos* (blog), July 28, 2013. http://www.patheos.com/blogs/johnbeckett/2013/07/a-pagan-view-of-compassion.html.

Benedict, Gerald, ed. *Buddhist Wisdom: The Path to Enlightenment*. London: Watkins Publishing, 2013.

Bonewits, Isaac. "What Do Neopagan Druids Believe?" Edited by Ian Corrigan in 2013. Ár nDraíocht Féin: A Druid Fellowship. Last modified April 19, 2014. https://www.adf.org/about/basics/beliefs.html.

Epstein, Joe. "The Wisdom of Native Americans." Mediate.com. July 2007. http://www.mediate.com/articles/epsteinj7.cfm.

Eusoff, Sultan. "The Centrality of Compassion in Islam." Speech given at the Sea of Faith Conference, Wellington, New Zealand, October 1, 2008. http://www.iman.co.nz/sultan_compassion_speech.php.

Holy Bible. New International Version. BibleGateway.com. Colorado Springs, CO: Biblica, 2011.

Johnson, Dave. "The Golden Rule." Life, Hope & Truth. Accessed April 8, 2016. http://lifehopeandtruth.com/change/christian-conversion/the-sermon-on-the-mount/the-golden-rule/.

Kindlers of the Sacred Rhythms. "Five Pagan Virtues." SacredRhythms.org. Accessed April 8, 2016. http://www.sacred rhythms.org/5virtues.php.

Kornberg Greenberg, Yudit. *Encyclopedia of Love in World Religions*, Volume 1. Santa Barbara, CA: ABC-CLIO, 2008.

Piburn, Sidney. *The Dalai Lama: A Policy of Kindness.* Delhi, India: Motilal Banarsidass, 2002.

What-When-How. "Compassion in Judaism." The-Crankshaft Publishing. Accessed April 8, 2016. http://what-when-how .com/love-in-world-religions/compassion-in-judaism/.

White, Brian, and Ven S. Dhammika. "BuddhaNet Basic Buddism Guide: A Five Minute Introduction." BuddhaNet Dharma Education Association & BuddhaNet. 2013. http://www.buddhanet.net/e-learning/5minbud.htm.

Day 25

Bullock, Janis R. "Bullying among Children." *Childhood Education* 78, no. 3 (2002): 130–33. doi:10.1080/00094056.200 2.10522721.

Diamond, Adele, and Kathleen Lee. "Interventions Shown to Aid Executive Function Development in Children 4–12 Years Old." *Science* 333, no. 6045 (August 2011): 259–64. doi:10.1126/science.1204529.

Mercree, Amy Leigh. "#BullyingNoWay—Facts, Bystander Behavior, and How to Help." *Fresh Talk with Amy Leigh Mercree*. YouTube video, 8:36. May 26, 2015. https://www.youtube.com/watch?v=ZN-dEHyBpoo.

NoBullying.com. "Bullying Statistics, The Ultimate Guide!" October 23, 2016. http://nobullying.com/bullying-statistics/.

To Write to the Author

If you wish to contact the author or would like more information about this book, please write to the author in care of Llewellyn Worldwide Ltd. and we will forward your request. Both the author and publisher appreciate hearing from you and learning of your enjoyment of this book and how it has helped you. Llewellyn Worldwide Ltd. cannot guarantee that every letter written to the author can be answered, but all will be forwarded. Please write to:

Amy Leigh Mercree
℅ Llewellyn Worldwide
2143 Wooddale Drive
Woodbury, MN 55125-2989

Please enclose a self-addressed stamped envelope for reply,
or $1.00 to cover costs. If outside the U.S.A., enclose
an international postal reply coupon.

Many of Llewellyn's authors have websites with additional information and resources. For more information, please visit our website at http://www.llewellyn.com.

GET MORE AT LLEWELLYN.COM

Visit us online to browse hundreds of our books and decks, plus sign up to receive our e-newsletters and exclusive online offers.

- **Free tarot readings • Spell-a-Day • Moon phases**
- **Recipes, spells, and tips • Blogs • Encyclopedia**
- **Author interviews, articles, and upcoming events**

GET SOCIAL WITH LLEWELLYN

Find us on
Facebook
www.Facebook.com/LlewellynBooks

Follow us on
twitter
www.Twitter.com/Llewellynbooks

GET BOOKS AT LLEWELLYN

LLEWELLYN ORDERING INFORMATION

Order online: Visit our website at www.llewellyn.com to select your books and place an order on our secure server.

Order by phone:
- Call toll free within the U.S. at 1-877-NEW-WRLD (1-877-639-9753)
- Call toll free within Canada at 1-866-NEW-WRLD (1-866-639-9753)
- We accept VISA, MasterCard, American Express and Discover

Order by mail:
Send the full price of your order (MN residents add 6.875% sales tax) in U.S. funds, plus postage and handling to: Llewellyn Worldwide, 2143 Wooddale Drive Woodbury, MN 55125-2989

POSTAGE AND HANDLING
STANDARD (U.S. & Canada):
(Please allow 12 business days)
$30.00 and under, add $4.00.
$30.01 and over, FREE SHIPPING.

INTERNATIONAL ORDERS:
$16.00 for one book, plus $3.00 for each additional book.

Visit us online for more shipping options.
Prices subject to change.

FREE CATALOG!

To order, call
1-877-
NEW-WRLD
ext. 8236
or visit our
website

Joyful
Living

101 WAYS TO TRANSFORM
YOUR SPIRIT & REVITALIZE
YOUR LIFE

AMY LEIGH MERCREE

Joyful Living
101 Ways to Transform Your Spirit and Revitalize Your Life
Amy Leigh Mercree

Experience joy each day and equip yourself for the ups and downs of life with *Joyful Living*, a practical roadmap to achieving inner and outer happiness. Using a mindful and balanced approach, Amy Leigh Mercree presents over a hundred ways to enliven your spirit and step into the blissful life you desire. Featuring affirmations, exercises, inspirational stories, and more, *Joyful Living's* uplifting entries are easy to use and can be enjoyed in any order. Explore a variety of themes from spiritual ecstasy to attitudes of gratitude to creative inspiration. Apply mindfulness techniques and work toward greater awareness of the present moment. With this book's guidance, you can calm your busy life and focus on the joyful world around you.

978-0-7387-4659-3, 360 pp., 5 x 7   **$16.99**

compassion
is the **key** to
everything

Find Your Own Path

ALEXANDRA CHAURAN

Compassion is the Key to Everything
Find Your Own Path
ALEXANDRA CHAURAN

Transform the way you interact with the world around you using *Compassion is the Key to Everything*, a practical, nondenominational book on discovering and exemplifying your own idea of what it means to be a compassionate person. Alexandra Chauran provides a guide to creating your personal code of ethics and integrating compassion into your life and community.

Explore your life's purpose, nurture a peaceful existence, and strengthen your relationships with this book's guidance on finding your own path. And unlike other books or spiritual programs that espouse specific diets or purchasing choices, *Compassion is the Key to Everything* provides insights that are adaptable to any lifestyle. Through exercises, meditations, and more, you'll learn to stop judging yourself and others and start making the world a better place.

978-0-7387-4667-8, 240 pp., 5 x 7   **$15.99**

THE
MINDFULNESS
HABIT

Six Weeks to Creating
the Habit of Being Present

KATE SCIANDRA

The Mindfulness Habit

Six Weeks to Creating the Habit of Being Present
Kate Sciandra

This step-by-step book offers a demystified and non-time-consuming approach to being present. It addresses the difference between meditation and mindfulness, why mindfulness is important, and dispels common misconceptions about the process. It then takes a step-by-step approach to not only teach exercises and techniques for developing mindfulness, but also includes instructions for finding the everyday opportunities to put them in place. This is done in a way that uses habit-forming prii   eks, you have both a tool kit

                                    understand the value of
livi   ty ways to create the habit
of   lness. In each section of
the   about a variety of topics,
exe   ng mindful habits in your
life

978-0-7387-4189-5, 216 pp., 5 x 7   **$16.99**